PLATO AND ARISTOPHANES

SERIES EDITOR

John Russon

REREADING ANCIENT PHILOSOPHY

PLATO AND ARISTOPHANES

Comedy, Politics, and the Pursuit of a Just Life

MARINA MARREN

NORTHWESTERN UNIVERSITY PRESS • EVANSTON, ILLINOIS

Northwestern University Press
www.nupress.northwestern.edu

Printed in the United States of America

10 9 8 7 6 5 4 3 2 1

Library of Congress Cataloging-in-Publication Data

Names: Marren, Marina, author.
Title: Plato and Aristophanes : comedy, politics, and the pursuit of a just life / Marina Marren.
Other titles: Rereading ancient philosophy.
Description: Evanston, Illinois : Northwestern University Press, 2022. | Series: Rereading ancient philosophy | Includes bibliographical references.
Identifiers: LCCN 2021027789 | ISBN 9780810144187 (paperback) | ISBN 9780810144194 (cloth) | ISBN 9780810144200 (ebook)
Subjects: LCSH: Plato. Republic. | Aristophanes—Criticism and interpretation. | Political science—Philosophy. | Greek drama (Comedy)—Political aspects—History and criticism.
Classification: LCC PA4279.R7 M37 2022 | DDC 320.011—dc23
LC record available at https://lccn.loc.gov/2021027789

for NNK and SDW

Nothing reveals our character more than
that which we find laughable.
—Johann Wolfgang von Goethe

CONTENTS

ACKNOWLEDGMENTS

I finished the first draft of this book during the winter of 2018–19 when my husband and I stayed in Athens. Our little, poorly heated, but charming rental apartment overlooked the roofs of the Koukaki district that would light up every evening with the brilliant colors of the setting sun. There wasn't a single day when Athens was not beautiful. My writing sped along, inspired by our frequent visits to the Archeological and the Cycladic Museums; by our walks to the Acropolis and Kerameikos; and by our trips to Sounion and to Delphi. The near-final version of the book was finished a year later, during my visit to Crete. This book is a tribute to Greece. To the Greek people, the Greek culture, and the extraordinary history of the many ancient peoples, places, and cultures that came together and made possible what we—today—refer to as the Greek Golden Age.

I am deeply grateful to my anonymous readers for their insightful and nuanced comments that helped improve this work. I am also very grateful to my editor, Trevor Perri, for his expertise and support, as well as to the Faculty Editorial Board of the Northwestern University Press for their interest in my work. For their congeniality, kindness, and support of my projects, I thank the "biggest little philosophy department" at the University of Nevada, Reno, where I have been teaching while preparing this book for publication.

For his unfailing friendship, expert advice, and his terrific book on *Philosophy and Comedy: Aristophanes, Logos, and Eros* (2008), I thank Bernard Freydberg. I am indebted to John Sallis. I am one of John's many students, who are deeply grateful to him for his extraordinary ideas and his many excellent books, including those on ancient Greek philosophy. I thank Fr. Gary Gurtler for his probing questions and uplifting sense of humor. I am grateful to Candace Hetzner, who is a mentor and a friend. I am also grateful to William Wians for years of collegial friendship and our most illuminating conversations about ancient Greek philosophy. I would like to thank Andrew Cutrofello, who has been my mentor for over a decade and whose erudition, sense of ethics, and dedication to the profession, his colleagues, and his students I strive to emulate. I am also grateful to Drew A. Hyland for his insightful work on Plato's comedy, and the clarity with which he does away with Plato's so-called "Theory of Forms" in his book on *Finitude and Transcendence in the Platonic Dialogues* (1995). Likewise, I am grateful to

Arlene Saxonhouse, Shane Montgomery Ewegen, Jacob Howland, Michael Vickers, Louis Ruprecht, Deborah Achtenberg, Mauro Bonazzi, and Ronna Burger for their work on ancient Greek philosophy, which has informed and shaped my own. I am especially grateful for decades of friendship with Stuart D. Warner. Stuart introduced me to the ideas of Seth Benardete, which became absolutely essential to my own understanding of the ancient Greeks, and to my engagement with the work of Leo Strauss, and especially with Strauss's *Socrates and Aristophanes* (1996) (pace Pierre Destrée and anyone else for whom Strauss and his writings are anathema). I am deeply grateful to Jason Wirth for his friendship, his advice, and the many conversations we had about philosophy. I thank my husband and my best friend, Kevin Marren, who is brilliant and true.

For their love of literature and their devotion to their students, I am forever grateful to Natalja Nikolaevna Kulman and Stuart D. Warner, to both of whom this book is dedicated.

PLATO AND ARISTOPHANES

INTRODUCTION

Philosophical Comedy as an Aesthetic Critique of Political Ideals

> Shame is the law's expression of man's ignorance by way of prohibition. The law completes man by saying no to man. The law clothes man and thus turns philosophy—man's awareness of his own ignorance—into shame.
>
> —Seth Benardete

Comedies—ancient and contemporary—often deal with politically charged practical questions. Some persistent questions are: How to dampen the kind of overly idealistic and zealously romantic view of life that supports a tyrant's rise to power? How to dispel the myopic allure of a self-satisfied life that sometimes enables and, at other times, embodies the tyrant? The answer the present book gives is that we do so by cultivating a love of humor in education and in social mores.

This book offers an interrogation of the political ideals and ideas in Plato's *Republic*—a foundational work of political philosophy. In the final analysis, my conclusion is that political tyranny feeds as much on hedonism and avarice as it does on zealotry and idealism. The *Republic* straightforwardly condemns the "dissipation" and "pleonexia" of a tyrant. However, Plato's attack on political idealism is more covert than these outright condemnations. One of the reasons for this is the double register of Plato's writing, which is both solemn and comedic. Plato draws on the same comedic stock and the same tropes as Aristophanes's comedy. Meanwhile, a number of Aristophanes's plays scoff at and bring into the light the political corruption in ancient Athens that serves as the backdrop of Plato's dialogues. The implication of Plato's aesthetic affinity for the comedic genre is that the study of political comedy clears the way for a philosophical revaluation of such notions as the "best regime," "perfect equality," and the "philosopher-king."

My analysis of Plato's political philosophy in the *Republic* follows the conceptual tradition, which claims that the pursuit of the common good and justice is premised on self-examination.[1] As my contribution to this school of thought, I argue that any worthwhile self-reflection goes hand in hand with the capacity to bring to light one's own shortcomings and flaws. The conversation that my research strikes up between Aristophanes's comedy and Plato's philosophy prompts the readers to question their own individual convictions, and it is meant to rejuvenate one's personal search for communal justice.

In this book, I carry out the interrogation of politics in the *Republic* through the comedic lens of Aristophanes's humor. The preparatory chapter 1 establishes the philosophical value of correspondences between the comedic elements in Plato's writing and Aristophanes's comedy. In chapter 2, I rely on Aristophanes's *Assembly Women* in order to play up the pitfalls of the communist utopia in *Republic* V. The conclusion to chapter 2 explains why a certain kind of democratic ideal is the obverse side of the same coin that holds a communist ideal, and how these two ideals both pave the way for tyranny. In chapter 3, I put pressure on the idea that the demagogues, sophists, and avaricious leaders are the only ones to blame for the troubles of a democratic state. To this end, I use my analysis of the *Knights* to argue for the culpability of the demos in *Republic* VI. In chapter 4, I expose the precariousness of the philosopher-king and show the insidious character of the metaphysical ideal that supports his rule. I advance my analysis by establishing concrete parallels between *Republic* VI and the *Birds*. In summary, the critique in this book first dismantles the romantic notion of absolute equality (chapter 2) as it pertains to Plato's thought. Then I go on to argue against the introduction of state management agendas according to which the general prosperity of the population safely alleviates the need for political participation (chapter 3). Lastly, I present the deleterious effects of the desire to be excused from politics in hopes of a simpler, less demanding; and a less litigious life (chapter 4). Chapter 5 serves as a focused discussion of tyranny that draws on my conclusions about the incendiary nature of certain mercenary and idealistic inclinations. Also in chapter 5, I argue that tyranny and self-examination are diametrically opposed. On the basis of this opposition, I conclude that we can find an antidote to tyranny in examining ourselves, while the practice of self-reflection finds aid in comedy. My conclusion to the entire book recommends that despite the possible dangers of addressing our pressing political concerns through the lens of comedy, this lighthearted attitude allows us to distance ourselves from our hard-won political commitments. If we do that, we are already better positioned to examine our own political views, as well as the general landscape of political action as it shapes our lives.

CHAPTER 1

Plato's and Aristophanes's Comedy

Why Comedy?

Actions of life, philosophical reflection, and theatrical drama are entwined—especially for the ancient Athenians in the fifth and fourth centuries B.C.E. This is another reason why comedy, as it perforates idealistic sentiments (however justified a given sort of idealism may be) and as it induces self-ridicule, is much more serious and more important to philosophy than first meets the eye. Comedy gives to us signs of a tragic future, a future that always follows suit, unless we curb our enthusiasm for self-aggrandizement—whether we seek to achieve that ambitious goal as members of a nationalistically minded group or state; as power-hungry individuals; or as self-important critics of ideas that do not agree with our ingrained points of view. Comic self-ridicule is a practice attendant upon our capacity to know ourselves. Self-knowledge necessitates, among other things, being able to publically acknowledge our less attractive and less laudable characteristics. Comedy serves as an impetus for this kind of knowledge because while laughing at the blunders and ignorance of the comedic characters, we are also invited to laugh at similar limitations and faults that we may find within ourselves. However, in order to be able to laugh at our own shortcomings, we must be open to the idea that every now and again the joke might be at our expense. This is not easy to do but it is necessary; especially at times of political crisis when nationalism, bigotry, zealotry, and corruption threaten to cut us off from justice and drown out any meaningful political participation.

Ancient Greek comedy, and especially Aristophanes's comedy, offer us an occasion to reflect not only on the world of politics in the fifth and fourth centuries B.C.E., but also on our own political realities. Although Aristophanes often has particular historical figures in mind (Cleon in the *Knights*, Alcibiades in the *Clouds*)[1] against whom he directs his comedic ire, the characters in his comedies are not simply exact copies of those persons. Instead, Aristophanes's characters are artistically rendered representations of types of human beings and, consequently, of the persistent flaws and vices that these types exhibit. Thus, Aristophanes's humor still has its bite for us today.

This book does not offer a theory of comedy. Any attempt to distill a theory of Aristophanes's comedy in order to find it in or apply it to Plato, from my point of view, misses the point of both Aristophanes's and Plato's art.[2] For this reason, but also because I wish to leave a space open for my readers to examine and to discover for themselves the most convincing points of contact between Plato and Aristophanes, I will refrain from giving summary accounts of the supposed theoretical affinities between Plato's and Aristophanes's plots based on their structure.[3] Theoretical accounts prescribe certain lines along which texts and ideas must be compared. However, neither Plato nor Aristophanes had any such theories about each other's work ready to hand.[4]

Aristophanic comedy unfolds as a theatrical performance. The plot (*muthos*), the characters (*ethos*), and the action (*praxis*, *dran*)[5] take place on stage. The *Clouds* or the *Birds*, the *Knights* or the *Lysistrata* are each a staged act. This matters for our appreciation of the jokes and our understanding of the aesthetic and philosophical value of these works. Aristophanes's comedy (the subject matter of the plays, the use of comedic themes, and the interplay between the speeches and the actions) serves as a guide in our detection and interpretation of the comedy in Plato's dialogues. Drew A. Hyland makes a conceptual connection between the dialogues and the comedic plays. He writes: "It is striking how pervasive is the agonistic element in the dialogues. Of the four forms of agon Cornford explicitly mentions as characteristic of comedy, three are plainly present in various dialogues."[6] Hyland goes on to point out that "the agon of life and death is central to the *Apology, Crito, Phaedo*, and even *Theatetus*; the agon of youth and old age is obviously present in those dialogues which Socrates has with youths, such as the *Lysis*, *Charmides*, and *Theatetus*, but also in Socrates's youthful encounter with Parmenides in the *Parmenides*."[7]

The common themes shared by the dialogical agons and the agons in comedy represent the behaviors and responses typical of perennial human dilemmas. These are, for example, the relationship between old and new (customs, mores, and laws), conflicting religious beliefs and different attitudes toward religion, as well as competing views on education, government, and what constitutes the best human life. My book articulates the correspondence between some such concerns in Plato's *Republic* and in Aristophanes's plays. I regard Aristophanes's comedies with the same attentiveness to their speculative dimension that I give to Plato's dialogues. In this way, relying on the extant research about the structure of ancient Greek comedy, my analysis proceeds by way of establishing thematic, poetic, and conceptual affinities between Plato and Aristophanes, as well as by seeking out similarities between Plato's and Aristophanes's poetic images.

Having said this, I admit that Plato's dialogues draw on a much greater variety of dramatic tropes and techniques than Aristophanes's comedies do. For one, although Aristophanes's comedies may refer to recognizable deities and their escapades, the comedic plots in his plays do not depend on the mythical stories that the ancient Greek audience would have readily recognized. It is not the comedians, but the tragedians who weave their dramas out of the stock of popular myths (e.g., Euripides's *Bacchae*, Sophocles's *Oedipus*, Aeschylus's *Prometheus Bound*). Similarly, the mythical and tragic elements of Plato's *Republic* enrich its philosophical meaning. The focus of my analysis can be made sharper through an investigation of tragic elements and motifs. For instance, *Republic* books VII–IX offer a sustained account of tyranny and also contain references to tragedy and tragic poets (550c, 562c, 568b).[8] As a political regime, tyranny is tragic because of the suffering it brings to both the ruler and the ruled. The blindness of the tyrant to her faults is also at the core of a tragic figure's blindness, which acts as a catalyst and drives the story of her life into the hands of a horrific fate. The fate of the tragic hero sharply poses the questions of retribution and of justice. These questions are very much alive in Plato's dialogues. All of this is to say that I recognize the serious and even the tragic tenor that is a part of Plato's literary style. Nonetheless, there are several reason why I seek to articulate Plato's political concerns through an analysis of Aristophanes's comedy.

Whereas the seriousness of tragedy and its capacity to appeal to our sense of justice is not a contested matter, the power of comedy as a form of aesthetic critique of politics is hardly a closed case. However, the idea that humor is incapable of igniting serious reflection or that comedy is inherently unphilosophical falls apart if we give our attention to Plato's use of comedy and to his dialogical engagement with Aristophanes's works.[9] Another reason why I pursue comedy as a path to understanding Plato's political philosophy is because I wish to contest another criticism of the comedic genre, which blames political satire for its dismissive attitude toward politics.[10] However, the central idea that guides my investigation is this: whereas tragedy is a genre that edifies our view of life, comedy deflates idealistic sentiments and glory-seeking predilections, which is important if we want to think about a just life. By a "just" life I do not mean a life that advocates patriotism, pushes political agendas, wields political power, or seeks to leave a legacy of glory and grandeur. Instead, my reading of the *Republic*—a reading that pursues the question of justice through the lens of comedy—is in step with the view that "the action of the *Republic* can be said to consist in first arousing spiritedness or the virtue belonging to it, that is to say, zeal dedicated to non-understood justice, that is, what we now mean by political idealism, and then in purging it."[11] The philosophical pertinence of comedy in the *Republic* resides not only in its capacity to ridicule corrupt desires, but also in its power to explode political ideals from within, while—at the same time—making us wonder why we thought those ideals to be desirable in the first place.

Plato relies on sophistical maneuvers, on poetry, on history, on what we today would call the "natural sciences," as well as on pre-Socratic thought, epos, myth, tragedy and comedy. However, at the end of the day he composes philosophical works. Thus, Plato has a much wider scope as a writer than Aristophanes. Nonetheless, this does not detract from my project but instead gives it focus. Where appropriate, I make observations about tragic and sophistic as well as mythical and poetic elements of Plato's art, but the focus of my investigation in this book remains comedy and politics in Aristophanes and in Plato. More specifically, the question that I ask is: What can we learn about ancient Greek (and especially fifth- and fourth-century Athenian) political ideas, ideals, and dealings by subjecting politics to the critique of comedic laughter? I argue that this study will also help us let comedy interrogate our own political commitments; that is, those political views and ideals that we hold dear today.

One of the main reasons why comedy is particularly well suited as a means of political critique is because, whereas politics busies itself with presenting coherent ideologies and action plans, comedy thrives on exposing the incoherence in our life. Aristophanes's jokes often turn on the exhibition of the incongruous elements (in the social order or in our personal beliefs) that otherwise might go unnoticed. These incongruous moments can be rather bawdy and perhaps even grating to our contemporary sensibility. Yet it is precisely this liminality of the genre that pushes the envelope and delicately walks the line that borders on the offensive, which makes comedy a powerful companion in both self-examination and political critique.

To give an example, in the *Assembly Women*, Aristophanes cleverly portrays the women as being well positioned to outsmart the men and seize power in Athens. The women, as Aristophanes portrays them, have a fighting chance at ruling the city because they have a natural inclination to be mounted during sex or to be on the bottom, which is exactly the trait of those men who are crafty at speaking (112–14). The crafty speakers—the orators, the public lawyers, the demagogues, and so on—hold power in Athens because of their capacity to convince those in the assembly and sway the people's support to their side. The men who hold power are also those who enjoy being overpowered and mounted by other men during sex. Needless to say, ancient Greeks were no strangers to homoerotic relations. This, then, is the scandalous moment: the men in power are the butt of the joke because of their sexual predilections. The women fare no better. Their political fate is staked *not* on their political aptitude, but on their dexterity in bed. One may dismiss Aristophanic humor for its lack of political correctness, but this unabashed bluntness is the point, of course. We could take offense at it, or we could ask ourselves whether and how Aristophanes's commentary on the unseemly political realities of the ancient Greeks also applies to us. The reason why it applies to Plato is because once we see that Plato's dialogues share certain themes and images with Aristophanes's plays, we can no longer take the interlocutors at their word, but must seek out the implications of the comedic moments. The incongruities in Plato's dialogues are somewhat more difficult to detect than they are in Aristophanes's plays, however. It is not immediately clear, for example, that the Kallipolis—the "best city" that the interlocutors construct in speech—is only beautiful in name."This is why, I argue, we must put Plato in dialogue with Aristophanes and thereby attune ourselves to comedy, without which philosophy falls away and we are left with dogma.

Just as on the stage, so too in Plato's writing, a comedic tenor qualifies and even reverses the straightforward meaning of an utterance or an exchange. The alteration in attitude—from serious to funny—that a successful comedy evokes in us has the advantage of playfully approaching such matters as religious convictions, ethical norms, social conventions, and political ideals (to name several subjects of serious inquiry). The aesthetic critique of which the comedian avails herself is a critique carried out not in the form of a treatise or an argument-based form, but in a way that raises serious questions playfully. This critique is powerful because it is not didactic. Comedy plants the seeds of questioning a given order (social, political, religious). It does so subversively and artfully. Comedy—if it is well received—ignites serious reflection and makes its appeal through laughter, which is pleasurable even if the ridicule is excessive. We enjoy a joke even if we feel the sting of shame and even if we cringe. Philosophy, and Plato undoubtedly knew this, is without a sting if it does not point out the incoherencies in our ideas, our lives, and perhaps most importantly, in ourselves. Comedy thrives on incongruity because what is funny is also somehow mismatched, out of order, and out of coincidence with our view of how the world ought to be if it is to be beautiful. It would be odd, given this presentation of comedy, if an exceptional thinker—Plato—did not resort to comedic scenes which, with undeniable insight and enviable precision, point out the ugliness to which all of us are subject.

Not only similarities between the themes of the agon and between the primary subject matters, but also direct references place Plato's and Aristophanes's works, conceptually, in close quarters. Socrates mentions Aristophanes in the *Apology* at 19c. The comedian appears as a character in the *Symposium*. The *Clouds*, although it never mentions Plato, gives Socrates one of the main roles. It is highly unlikely that Aristophanes's extant works respond to anything that Plato himself wrote. However, the fact that Plato in his dialogues openly features Aristophanes is clear, and that he less openly, but for that matter no less meaningfully, engages with Aristophanes's art (responds to it, echoes it, draws on it) is at least plausible.[12]

The dialogues deliver their philosophical meaning not only directly—through the interlocutors' speeches, but also less obviously—through the action of the various arguments in their exchanges. Seth Benardete says about Plato's literary technique that there is "in fact an argument in the action. If you don't see that, it just looks as if you have the repeated modification of a theme as the dialogue goes on. . . . The mistake is when you take the details of the dialogue as a constant modification of the themes of the dialogue. But the consequence is that nothing really changes."[13] However, there is a way to understand a dialogical development and its philosophical meaning not on the basis of a modular or linear modification of a theme, but dynamically, as one would understand a work of drama.[14] Benardete notes that this dynamic quality "turns out to be something that already was in Homer, and in tragedy. This was not something invented by Plato; he must have realized that they had done this very odd thing [whereby] . . . you get total incoherence of plot, which brings you immediately to what the deeper issue is."[15] On this view, it makes no sense to pursue apologetics that try to build "Plato's theories" at the expense of smoothing out the incongruous moments in his works. However, claims that chastise Plato's dialogues for their "faulty arguments" or "inconsequential myths" do not hold water either. Both staunch criticism and attempts at apologetics fail to get at Plato's meaning on account of utterly misunderstanding the *style* of Plato's art.

Plato's dialogues operate according to "a concept of truth" that calls for "the simultaneous truthfulness of different meanings and modes of reality."[16] The dialogues, in other words, share "a specific feature of ancient Greek tragedy that has much to do with Dionysus." Dionysus, as Renate Schlesier portrays the god, symbolizes the dramatic layering of masks. In addition to the mask that the actor in a tragedy or in a comedy would wear,[17] Schlesier explains, "a second mask is created verbally and thus . . . appears before the eyes of the spectators."[18] In terms of Plato's dialogues, Schlesier's thesis looks exactly like Benardete's insistence that "there [is] . . . an argument *in* the action."[19] Since we read the dialogues, instead of watching them as we would watch a captivating film or a theatrical performance, the verbal mask comes first. However, discursivity is not the only dialogical dimension. The dramatic layering of masks is preserved. There is a difference between what the dialogical exchanges say and what is carried out or done by means of these exchanges. A line from Plato accepts the same polyvalent truth as does a dramatic line. There is, for example, what Socrates says—there is the meaning of that uttered statement—and then there is the dialogical context that activates the speech, that gives it a performative dimension.[20] This is the action of the speech, and there is an argument "*in* the action."[21]

Comedy in Plato often has the function of indicating the movement of the dialogical action, which refracts the immediate meaning of Plato's lines. This issue of multiple meanings that the speeches in Plato's dialogues relate is part of the comedic genre. For instance, "ironic speech [is the] . . . speech wherein the truth is significantly other than, and in strong cases the opposite of, what is said."[22] Hyland draws this parallel between the multidimensional conception of truth in Plato's philosophizing and in life. He claims that the "structure of irony is not merely literary but philosophical in that it is founded in and revelatory of Plato's teaching about human nature. Human life is therefore deeply and inherently ironic."[23] With that we make a full account of the relationship between theater drama (and specifically comedy), the dramatic character of Plato's dialogues, and the *dramata* or actions of life. If irony (as Hyland tells us) and comedy (as Benardete says) are a part of the action of life, if there is irony in the dialogues, and if comedy furthers the action of Plato's philosophizing, then any interpretation of Plato that purports to have value for life has to include an interpretation of Plato's comedy.

A History of Ancient Greek Comedy and Politics

Although "drama" is said of both tragedy and comedy in the present work, in fact, as Arthur Wallace Pickard-Cambridge tells us, "it is very doubtful whether δρᾶμα [*drama*] was ever used of comedy in classical Attic."[24] According to Pickard-Cambridge, it is "at least possible that δρᾶμα [*drama*] was originally a Doric word."[25] Consequently, "δρᾶν [*dran*] is primarily in Attic a word with a religious colour, and is used especially of serious and solemn religious performances."[26] With regard to comedy, Pickard-Cambridge continues, "there can be no doubt that κωμῳδία [*kômôdia*] is connected with κῶμος [*kômos*] (κομάζειν) [*komadzein*] [revel], not with κώμη [*kômê*], and that in any case κώμη [*kômê*] was a good Attic word, at least in the fifth century B.C.E., though it referred to a quarter of the city, not to a country town or village."[27] Pickard-Cambridge's analysis denies to Aristotle the veracity of the report according to which "some say they [the imitations] are also called *dramata* because they imitate those doing [*drôntas*]."[28] Aristotle supposes that depending on its mode, "imitation" includes the art of Sophocles, Homer, and Aristophanes; namely tragedy, epos, and comedy. All three imitate "acting [*prattontas*] and doing [*drôntas*]."[29] Since the word for "doing" is Dorian in origin, Aristotle concludes that "it is for this reason that the Dorians also make a claim to tragedy and comedy."[30] However, Pickard-Cambridge insists that "drama" is not used to refer to comedy and places the origin of the name for the plays, which invoke laughter, decisively with "revelry." Aristotle is less definitive when he recites the possible origins of the term "comedy," saying that the "Dorians make the names the sign. For they say that they call their outlying districts villages [*kômai*], while the Athenians call them demes, as if comedians or revel singers [*kômôdoi*] were so called not from reveling [*kômazein*] but by wandering from village to village [*kata kômas*]."[31]

In tracing the activity in which the raucous displays and performances of comedy began, Roy C. Flickinger has recourse (by way of Aristotle) to Aristophanes himself. Flickinger, following Francis M. Cornford, takes up Aristophanes's *Acharnians*, a play where he finds "the best illustration"[32] of what Aristotle thinks is the beginning of comedic revelry, namely the "phallic ceremonies."[33] Flickinger recites the scene from the *Acharnians* in which the sacrifice to Dionysus is meant to celebrate the peace that the private citizen, Dicaepolis, "concluded . . . with Sparta."[34] Before long, "Dicaepolis re-forms his procession with various coarse remarks and starts up a phallic ballad of an obscene nature in honor of Phales. . . . The proceedings thus consist of a procession to the place of sacrifice, the sacrifice itself, and the phallic song."[35] There is a strong relationship between the Dionysian phallic procession and comedic revelry, and hence between comedy and Dionysus.[36] Aristophanes's plays are themselves a source to which the scholarship refers when working out the details of this relationship. The relationship between Dionysus and tragedy solidified in "534 B.C.E., when Pisistratus, tyrant of Athens, established a new festival . . . in honor of Dionysus Eleuthereus [and] . . . made a contest in tragedy the chief feature of its program."[37] Comedic performances joined the dramatic contest in 487/86 B.C.E.[38]

Pisistratus's festival, the City Dionysia, was meant to strengthen Athens, and the comedians gladly contributed to it. However, they understood their role in this strengthening in their own way. For instance, Aristophanes's comedies, which were featured both at the Athenian and the Lenaean Dionysia at the end of the fifth and the start of the fourth century, shine a light on the shortcomings and missteps of the city's leaders. The comedic banter of his plays does not fail to reach Pericles himself. Another target of Aristophanes's satire was a demagogue, Cleon.[39] This Athenian politician was so upset with the *Babylonians*, for instance, that he proceeded to sue the playwright. Pericles banned direct and virulent mockery in comedy after the revolt on Samos (440–439). The 438–437 ban did not last long, but that it was put in place at all attests to the revelatory and destabilizing potential of ancient Greek comedy. Pericles saw in it not only a capacity to undermine his own persona, but also to unhinge the power dynamics between the city-states. It is only plausible that this subversive force, of which Plato avails himself in his dialogues, turns a number of straightforward dialogical conclusions on their head.

The historical conditions that framed Plato's and Aristophanes's works—the corrupt machinations of Athenian politicians, tyranny, and the dusk of Athenian glory—informed both authors' interest in politics. Aristophanes's comedies draw on the unseemly realities of the Peloponnesian War (*Lysistrata*, *Acharnians*, and *Peace*); the petty politicking and demagoguery of corrupt statesmen (*Wasps*, *Knights*); the blunders of Athenian education (*Clouds* and, to some extent, *Frogs*); the self-centered greediness and narrow-mindedness of the Athenian majority (*Thesmophoriazusae*, *Plutos*); and the resultant failure of Athens to secure a reasonable political regime (*Assembly Women*, *Birds*). The interest that Aristophanes's comedies show in the political fate of Athens is apparent.

On my view, in Plato and in Aristophanes, the roots of political corruption cannot be placed squarely with one group of people or a single social class. Thus in the *Knights*, it is clear that the owner of the House of Athens, Demos, who is an image of the Athenian democratic majority, is as much to blame for the city's troubles as are its politicking and self-serving leaders. Similarly in *Republic* book VIII, the democratic citizens with their unlimited desire for freedom do not tolerate any limitations—not even the limits that are imposed by law. Their unhinged desire is the ground on which a tyrant can erect a cruel and unprincipled regime. The infighting of the ruling elite is a trope that both Aristophanes and Plato take up. Again in the *Knights*, we have an example of the squabbles not between the demos and the rulers, but *within* the ruling parties. The Paphlagonian tanner causes much distress to the attendants of Demos and fights the sausage seller (his political rival) in order to stay at the helm in the house of Demos, that is, in order to stay in power in Athens. These squabbles appear to be Aristophanes's metaphor for the inner disagreements and power struggles among the oligarchs.[40] My analysis in chapter 3 shows how Plato's image of the ship of state (488a–489d) in *Republic* VI captures this struggle. The members of the ruling elite at Athens are no strangers to political rivalry, and Plato, of course, is aware of this.

Historically, Pisistratus secured his power by relying on the support of and marrying into the well-established aristocratic family of the Alcmaeonids. Despite or perhaps because of Pisistratus's success, the Alcmaeonids saw in him a rival. I will address this rivalry in the context of tyranny in *Republic* VIII–IX, which I examine in chapter 5. However, for now, suffice it to say that Athenian tyrants did not only usurp power by wresting it from the democratic majority; they also advanced their interests by pitting the demos against the aristocratic elite. This pattern can be seen in *Republic* VIII–IX, where the tyrant takes advantage of the democratic majority and, at the same time, seeks to eliminate any member of the ruling elite who dares to oppose him (567a–568a). Political violence among the members of the elite is also an idea that is alive in the *Birds*—the play that I examine in conjunction with my further study of *Republic* VI. In the play, as soon as Peisthetairos becomes the ruler, his trusty companion Euelpides leaves the scene. Given the cruelty with which Peisthetairos treats the denizens of the newly founded city and even the gods, we can assume that his all but ostracized comrade, Euelpides, had little chance at being a co-regent.

Tyranny in Plato's and Aristophanes's works does not mimic, but refracts the historical tyrants and their ways. This refraction means that sometimes the actions of various historical rulers are amalgamated into a single image or conceptual trope. Alternatively, in the case of the *Republic*, books VIII–IX separate out the different political denominations that are entwined in life. Socrates presents a neat and linear relationship between the regimes, progressing from supposedly the best kind to the worst. However, these regimes represent the various rival factions that operated simultaneously in Greek history. For instance, the oligarchs appointed by the Spartans when Athens lost the Peloponnesian War acted tyrannically against the democrats, as well as against some well-established members of the aristocracy. However, as I already indicated, earlier in the history of Athens it was Pisistratus—a member of the aristocratic elite—who was dubbed a "tyrant." Keeping such historical details in mind, I extrapolate and posit that virtually no one is immune to tyrannical inclinations. These inclinations are especially potent in us when we hold power over others. Even a modicum of power, such as the dialogical interlocutors have over the construction and the denizens of the (supposedly) ideal city in speech, is liable to call up unseemly feelings and desires. I show how this is the case regarding the interlocutors when I discuss *Republic* VI by amplifying the tyrannical motifs through a study of the *Birds*. Neither Plato's characters, nor we today are in safe waters if we claim to have purged all tyranny from our lives. In view of this, and if we care about justice, it is all the more necessary to place ourselves in conversation with Plato's dialogues.

Remarks about Plato's Style

Plato composes his dialogues out of arguments (both plausible and faulty) and presents those dialogues by stylized (even if often historical) characters, but that is hardly all he does. In no case, at least as far as the dialogues are concerned, do we read Plato's "direct reporting" on a subject—whether that subject is piety, excellence, rhetoric, justice, beauty, eros, and so on. Instead, the dialogues are Plato's artistic appropriation of these subjects.[41] As much as the dialogues are works of philosophy, they are also works of literature, and as a literary author Plato is no stranger to theater drama, that is, to tragedy and comedy. If we seek to understand the dialogues as works of literature that have a dramatic structure, then we should keep in mind the noncoincidence between the speeches of the dialogical characters and the ideas of the author. What does this mean? This means that just as we would find it odd and false to take, say, Raskolnikov to be the spokesman for Dostoevsky or Khlestakov's utterances to be Gogol's telegraphed ideas, so too, we should dismiss as preposterous the claim that any of the characters ever simply say what Plato truly thinks.

Leo Strauss notes that this view of Plato's dialogues, which bars us from reading Plato's own ideas off of any of the speeches that the dialogical interlocutors exchange, is "paradoxical." However, those paradoxes with which Plato's texts are replete throw a wrench into common, accepted understanding of the subject matter and thereby ignite—or at least can ignite—thought. Strauss admits that "no doubt it is paradoxical to say that an utterance of the Platonic Socrates is no more revealing of Plato's thought than the quoted utterance of Macbeth is of the thought of Shakespeare."[42] This admission is a rhetorical ploy on Strauss's part, just as Socrates's admission of ignorance is a rhetorical ploy of Plato. If we admit it as a conclusion, we have completely missed the point, because as a paradoxical statement, it is the first step—a premise—on the basis of which we conduct the ensuing investigation. For Strauss, the paradox amounts to a realization that there is a much greater affinity between Plato's dialogues and Shakespeare's plays, for instance, than there is between what Socrates says and what Plato thinks. Although we cannot dream of figuring out the latter (Plato's meaning) without having the former (Socrates's words as they are penned by Plato), the two are not one and the same. How to read Plato? Strauss recommends that we take seriously the dialogues' dramatic structure. He writes of Shakespeare's tragedy, which like Plato's dialogues is composed of both words and actions, that "perhaps the action of the play refutes Macbeth's utterances. Perhaps the dramatic poet reveals his thought exclusively by the play as a whole, by the action, and not by speech, that is to say, the speeches of his characters. This much we can say safely," Strauss asserts, "that the distinction between speeches and deeds, and the implication that the deeds are more trustworthy than the speeches, is basic for the understanding of works like the Platonic dialogues. The deeds are the clue to the meaning of the speeches."[43]

The philosophical meaning of the dialogues must be gleaned or even deduced from the drama—the deeds or actions of the characters—and the speeches (the *logoi* and the *muthoi)*. It is detective work that we carry out as readers, or to follow Derrida's insightful formulation, as viewers of the dialogical text.[44] The dialogical circumstances of the text, call it the "scene," are comprised of both the actions and the speeches. We need to set the two against each other in order to understand anything about either one of the pair. In his text "The Origins of Political Science and the Problem of Socrates," Strauss notes that the "poets possess genuine knowledge of the soul . . . poetry is *psychologia kai psychagogia*, understanding of the soul and guiding of the soul, . . . just as Platonic philosophy itself, for not every philosophy is psychology in the Platonic sense."[45] To guide the soul is not the same as to instruct it. Instruction may prescribe certain moral tenets, expound conclusions, or instill in the soul appreciation for attractive, though in the case of Platonist ideas, for example, rather questionable theories. Hyland explains that the proponents of the theory of Ideas

> begin with . . . an unjustified assumption, the imposition of rather late modern measures of philosophy as necessarily systematic (therefore containing a set of "theories," technical terminology, and so on), measures that not only are not acknowledged in the dialogues themselves, but are even antithetical to the dialogue form in which Plato has chosen to present his thinking to the public.[46]

To Hyland, the dialogical form indicates the fact that we are mistaken if we take Plato to be a systematic thinker who seeks to offer to the world a set of instructive theories. Such a mistake, in Hyland's view, has deleterious consequences. I agree with his assessment. In chapter 4, I offer a reflection on the unwelcome effects of imposing a mold upon Plato's texts. Such a mold can produce some single theory or some definitive system of philosophy—be it political, metaphysical, or moral. However, the dialogical action undermines whatever theory might be concluded from the characters' words. The action, as Strauss's student Benardete reiterates, also contains an argument. Derrida suggests that the reading which produces theories, but relegates the drama to the fringes, is a myopic reading. It depreciates the playfulness of Plato's text, which Freydberg shows is crucial to following its meaning.[47] The stringently theoretical approach to Plato's playful philosophizing is unduly limited, one-sided, headstrong, and too sure of itself to be careful, and therefore it is bound to be self-undermining.

Freydberg, following Sallis, sees Plato as an author who weaves philosophy with, or rather out of, play.[48] Sallis develops intricate analyses of dialogical play and its consequences for Plato's philosophy throughout his seminal text *Being and Logos: Reading the Platonic Dialogues*. From the start of his engagement with the *Republic*, Sallis stresses for us the conceptual and interpretive significance of play. He determines the reason why we must attune ourselves to Plato's dialogical play when reading the *Republic*. It has to do with the fact that "the *Republic* is so thoroughly assimilated not only to the tradition of interpretation but also to the philosophical tradition at large that to attempt to gain an originary access to it seems almost like trying to jump over one's own shadow."[49] The ingrained views that the history of this dialogue's reception passes on to new readers have to be—somehow—resisted. If they are, then the text can speak to us anew or, as Sallis writes, it can show its "originary" meaning to us. Following Sallis's recommendation, I approach the *Republic* by paying careful attention to its playful elements and, especially, to the playfulness of Plato's comedy. Not only is there playful content—plentiful playful passages and specific passages about play (*Phaedrus* 277e, *Statesman* 268e, *Republic* 536e–537a)—in Plato's dialogues, but also and no less importantly, their form, their dramatic structure, invites us to be playful; that is, to take part in Plato's play. Sallis quotes Jacob Klein, who recalls "Paul Friedländer's remark [that] '[t]he dialogue is the only form of book that seems to suspend the book form itself.'"[50] Klein says that this idea "could perhaps be elaborated on as follows: a (Platonic) dialogue has not taken place if we, the listeners or readers, did not actively participate in it."[51] My comment on this Russian-doll nestling of quotations is the following thesis: to us, the readers, there is no dialogue (i.e., the text remains inert) unless we listen, watch, and participate—that is, unless we play while reading Plato's writing. If we do play along, then the dialogue comes alive and gives to us the wondrous world of Plato's dramatic, dialogical philosophizing.

Comedy at Play

Comedy, which is a part of Plato's philosophical play (and a part of his literary style) puts pressure on the prescriptive tenor of the dialogues. Comedy redirects apparently serious passages and turns their initial meaning on its head. The straightforward meaning of the passages changes course when we read these through a comedic lens. Plato alternates the use of comedic characters—such as the overzealous, but not particularly bright Apollodorus, the Phalerian, in the *Symposium*, or the frustrated and self-important Cleitophon in the *Cleitophon*—with the employment of comedic sketches. Plato resorts to a dramatically and philosophically significant use of comedy in the *Republic*, the *Cratylus*,[52] and the *Charmides*. Comedy is mentioned in relation to self-knowledge in the *Philebus* (48c).[53] Aristophanes, the comic poet, "tells a funny story with a tragic message"[54] in the *Symposium*. Aristophanes is also mentioned, albeit in the somber context of the charges mounted against Socrates, in the *Apology*.

The *Republic* is a plentiful source of Plato's use of comedy. One of many examples where jokes are both made and mentioned comes up in the context of the guardians' education and equality in *Republic* V. In chapter 2 of the present work, I analyze the question of equality between the guardian women and men in view of similar innovations proposed by the main character of Aristophanes's *Assembly Women*. For now, I ask: can the passages about the absolute equality of the sexes and the ages—that is, about the kind of equality that also equalizes or dismisses the obvious differences of the body—be read straightforwardly, that is, prescriptively and not as a joke? For the sake of an experiment, let us say that they can be. In this case, Socrates's ideas about physical exercise (452a–c), for instance, suggest that it is needful to suppress shame if the guardians aspire to receive an equal and proper education. The kind of shame that Socrates means here arises when human beings are denuded in public and are exposed to other naked bodies (452c). Naked communal exercises further require a suppression of—or at least a temporary insensitivity to—erotic desire. Let us imagine—and this is what Socrates in the *Republic* recommends—that men and women (regardless of their sexual persuasion) exercise naked, and this is meant to be neither shameful, nor laughable, nor any longer uncomfortable. Instead, this naked communal exercise must be made into a custom. However, if this custom were to come to pass, then it would be needful to either learn how not to become sexually aroused while looking at naked bodies, or else to feel perfectly at ease with becoming excited. This would be a strange and, indeed, a supremely laughable spectacle—old women, young women, and all manner of men sweating, contorting, and play-fighting together.[55] And yet, Socrates advises that such a scene must not make us laugh (452d). If we take his recommendation seriously and follow it to its logical conclusion, then we run up against a situation in which physicality no longer means much for sexuality—for our erotic desires. We would perhaps return to an "original" androgynous state, which looks very much like the state of affairs described by the character Aristophanes in the *Symposium* (189d–190c).

In the *Symposium*, Plato has Aristophanes describe double male, double female, and male-female beings as perfect, self-contained unities who are self-sufficient to the point of being un-erotic. The beings in this story are so complete that sexual difference between them doesn't matter, nor is it necessary for their procreation (191b–c). Instead, sexual partnership is—fantastically—constituted within a single being (189e–190a, 191a–b). Aside from being inhumanly asexual, these beings are also extraordinarily hubristic (190b–c). Their hubris leads to their demise, which by and by and with divine assistance turns the globular entities into halves that we would recognize as human beings, more or less. Humanity brings with it pangs of longing, the pull of sexual desire, and the pains of procreation, as well as an incompleteness that weakens us. These make us feel a need for one another; they make us feel imperfect and ashamed. As if rewinding the arc of the events in Aristophanes's story, Socrates in the *Republic* calls for the sorts of changes in our attitude to sexuality and shame that—if they were possible—would make us superhuman, or perhaps impart to us an inhuman completeness.[56]

Even if it is entertained as an option for the biotechnologically enhanced future, the image conjured up by a straightforward reading of the *Symposium* passage hearkens the reader back to the spellbound origins of tragedy. If taken literally, the condition that Aristophanes's tale describes and which the limit-case interpretation of Socrates's speech in the *Republic* seems to prescribe is a tragic illusion.[57] This image seeks to recover an impossible, ideal state of things as if it were somehow an origin or a foundation of human life. But this desire to make a fantastical ideal manifest in life, as I conclude in chapter 2, leads to tragic consequences. The unrealistic image of naked communal exercise in the *Republic* also calls to mind Aristophanes's own writing and his scathing ridicule of outlandish ideas, such as those he lampooned in the *Clouds* (e.g., at lines 194 and 225).

In a spirit of nostalgic simplicity, we could follow Socrates's imperative "to be serious" (452c) and legislate that "the women [should be] exercising naked with the men" (452a). Alternatively, we could view the *Republic* passage as an opportunity to think about the meaning of Socrates's imperative, which states that "we mustn't be afraid of all the jokes" (452b). Put negatively, this excessive fearlessness is rash and thoughtless. If no joke is alarming, are we even capable of distinguishing between what is laughable and what is not? In a positive sense, the line suggests that we should set fear aside also, if not especially, when the joke is at our own expense. Excessive fearlessness in the face of being seen as a subject of comedy turns out to be the courage requisite for thinking about both the dialogical incongruities and those incongruities we find in ourselves. Attentiveness to Plato's comedy helps us take note and make sense of outlandish suggestions and faulty arguments, without trying to make them fit into some preconceived meaning or theory. This is especially pertinent when unpleasant idiosyncrasies are covered over by the promise of perfection—whether it be a promise of perfect equality, perfect knowledge, or a perfect image of oneself.

I propose that Plato's dialogues—often, if not most of the time—are read too literally, too seriously, and too self-assuredly, that is, too tragically.[58] All of my book, in some sense, is dedicated to offering a counterpoint to such tragic readings of the *Republic*. This pursuit comes to a head in chapter 5, in my discussion of humorless readings of the text and of the ensuing tyranny which such all-too-serious views of Plato's dialogues engender. For now, in a preparatory manner, I seek to understand the structure and meaning of Plato's own use of comedy.

Attunement to the Study of Comedy in the *Republic*—Glaucon's Case

Consider the passage from *Republic* VI that punctures (and if not deflates, then qualifies or reroutes) the speeches about the famous ascent to the Good (507a–509c).[59] At this precise point, which is traditionally interpreted as one of the *Republic*'s dialogical apexes (at lines 509a–c), the action of the speeches between Socrates and Glaucon undermines their high-minded tenor. Attentiveness to comedy—to the undertones of the exchanges—helps us follow the argument in the speech's action. At 508e–509a, Socrates solicits from Glaucon his view of what is great about the Good. Glaucon thinks that what places the good beyond knowledge and truth, making it greater than and a condition for both, is pleasure (509a). Upon hearing Glaucon's response, Socrates hushes him (*euphêmei*, 509b). Socrates takes Glaucon down a notch at this seemingly high point of their discussion because Glaucon exhibits an almost juvenile excitement about pleasure.

Why is this exchange between the dialogical characters of the *Republic* comical and funny? Socrates's speeches appear to instruct Glaucon to consider truth, knowledge, and the Good in order to curb his enthusiasm about pleasure. However, these speeches do not reach the desired result. What transpires is similar to an episode of the "Abbott and Costello Show" where Bud works at the bakery, but Lou is convinced that Bud loafs around. Likewise, the comedy in the ascent to the Good of the *Republic* is premised on the difference between what Socrates means for Glaucon to do and what Glaucon thinks Socrates means. The two meanings get confused because of what both characters, respectively, understand as the highest and best. Glaucon's own predilections and his unexamined desires skew his understanding. The bend, as Jacob Howland argues, is so drastic that it constitutes Socrates's inability to effect a change in Glaucon's fate.[60]

Note that Glaucon does not simply privilege the pleasurable things in life. He masks his preference for pleasure by aligning pleasure with beauty. Here is how he does it: "You speak of an overwhelming beauty . . . if it provides knowledge and truth but is itself beyond them in beauty. You surely don't mean it is pleasure" (509a). At this point Socrates responds: "Hush . . . Glaucon . . . consider its image still further" (509a). The Greek text, which begins with: "*amêchanon kallos . . . legeis*" (509a5), can also be translated as "you speak of an uncontrived beauty." Glaucon's focus on beauty is noticeable. Whereas Socrates does not mention beauty at all (at least not in the preceding eighteen lines, the most recent mention of it occurring at 491b), Glaucon uses the word "beauty" twice when he tries to guess the subject to which Socrates attributes "*meidzonôs timêteon*" (509a4), that is, "great honor." Glaucon guesses wrong. His mind is on "*hêdonê*" (509a6) or pleasure, and he is promptly hushed by Socrates.

Socrates's "*euphêmei*" (509a) means both "speak well" and "hush." Whatever the preferred translation, it is an imperative to be mindful of what is being expressed. But what is being expressed by Glaucon? Taken schematically, his expression equates whatever is most honorable with what is most beautiful, and he places pleasure above both. Given the clues that Glaucon misses, notably the suggestion that terms such as "good," "beautiful," "truth," and "knowledge" cannot simply be equated or substituted for one another, it is unlikely that Glaucon's understanding of a beautiful whole is synonymous with Aristotle's meaning in the *Poetics*,[61] or that Glaucon's relationship with pleasure is as meaningful as Aristotle's articulation thereof at the end of the *Nicomachean Ethics*.[62] Presumably, it is not the anachronistic application of the philosopher's thinking to Glaucon's ideas that is to blame for the fact that the latter are wanting in depth. The conversations about knowledge and truth—the kinds of conversations that Glaucon and Socrates are having in the sixth book of the *Republic*—are intensely pleasurable, from Aristotle's point of view. Yet, Glaucon does not comment on the pleasurable character of the exchanges with Socrates, but aims at securing some other pleasure outside of or above his dialogical dealings.

The unexamined desire that surfaces as Glaucon's excitement about pleasure comically undermines the ascending structure of the speeches about the Good (509a–c). If the pursuit of knowledge and truth, as well as the conversations about the Good, are carried out for the sake of securing the construction of and the ascent to the just regime, then Glaucon's view of pleasure's supremacy places this ascent on a rather questionable foundation.[63]

Plato's brother Glaucon is not yet seen by Plato's contemporaries as either the historical or literary Glaucon. He is remembered as the man who fought at Megara (the possible dates of the battle in question are discussed by Debra Nails)[64] and was a lover of the tyrannically minded Critias IV. Glaucon's excitement about valor and honor (the sorts of things that depend on one's *thumos*), his lively interest in pleasure (which eros undergirds), and his flirtations with tyrannical persons if not with tyranny, is thematized in Plato's stylized rendition of the man. Benardete holds that the "manly and erotic"[65] Glaucon picks up, modifies, and develops "Thrasymachus's account."[66] This means that Glaucon's character is one of the dialogical vehicles by means of which Plato sets up the relationship between tyranny and the analysis of the Good.[67]

The tragic drama in the dialogue presents Glaucon as wavering between his predilection for the kinds of pleasures that are accessible to powerful members of the polis and the benefits of searching for knowledge and truth. Glaucon's preferred enjoyment of financial support from the polis and his pleasure at receiving the many and choicest erotic partners are presented in the guise of the guardians' blessed life in book V at 464c and 468c.[68] Despite Socrates's consequent attempt to redirect Glaucon's desires away from such pleasures and toward wisdom (475b), it is still pleasure that Glaucon places above knowledge and truth. If Glaucon is supposed to be transformed in the course of his conversation with Socrates, the transformation does not take place at the time that the ascent to the Good is accomplished.

Why, then, does Glaucon bother with the construction of the just city and with figuring out what kind of citizen must be at the top? Rosen explains that Glaucon's concern with getting ahead is a result of his character as a citizen. For Rosen, Glaucon is "someone who aspires to political prominence."[69] Rosen supports his view of the character as someone who covets power in the polis by referring us to Xenophon's *Memorabilia*.[70] An aspiration to be the foremost man in the city is not problematic in its own right, but it turns out that in Glaucon's case, this prevents him from understanding the multivalent implications of the exchanges that he has with Socrates. Glaucon is blinded by too lively an interest in coming out on top. The ascent, in which book VI of the *Republic* ends, then, is rather a descent or—minimally—an enterprise that undoes itself for Glaucon in the process of its unfolding.

The signs of this tragicomedy, in which Glaucon (and perhaps the readers of the *Republic*) play key parts—the glimpses of the self-undermining dynamic at play in the seemingly most hopeful, most secure, and most important images that the dialogue offers—appear early. This trajectory, which terminates in the search for education as a power that will allow Glaucon to revel in pleasure, is set out in book II. Unsatisfied with the simple city or what Rosen refers to as the "true city,"[71] Glaucon calls for a life that does not exclude "relishes" (372c).[72] Toying with Glaucon, Socrates at first offers him literal relishes, the kinds of things that go well with hearty, simple food. In his impatience, Glaucon disparagingly identifies the simple city as the "city of sows" (372d).[73] The relishes that Glaucon has in mind are not "salt, olives, cheese . . . and onions" (372c), but "conventional" (372d) sophistications like "perfume . . . courtesans . . . poets . . . actors . . . beauticians . . . relish-makers and cooks" (373a–c) which intensify the pleasures of dwelling in the city and (sometimes truly, but often only seemingly) dignify human life. In response to Glaucon's request, Socrates continues to poke fun at him.

That Socrates's remarks are comic is evident not only from the tone of Plato's writing, but also in view of the fact that hunger, voraciousness, and cuisine predilections, in short, things related to food, were some of the favorite subjects of ancient Greek comedy. The topic of food preparation even informs the style of comedic presentation. In tracing the appearances of food in Astydamas's *Hercules*, Rebecca Lämmle observes how the "art of writing cooks up a metaphorical verse, which presents the poet serving his play to the audience as if it were a rich meal."[74] Socrates, too, spreads in front of Glaucon a feast to fall for. How could there be a city without relishes?! Even the simple city, which Socrates first describes, has wine. Is Glaucon, indeed, off point when he calls for sophistications and goes along with Socrates's metaphorically gastronomic innovations which transform the proposed city into an inflamed if not a corrupt one? If Glaucon is misled, then how and what does his confusion signify?

Glaucon interrupts Socrates's description of life in a simple city. He punctures the narrative. He gives a new beginning, or at least a new turn to the conversation. Glaucon's demand for a different image of a city originates from a disappointment. It is a negative impulse that urges him on. Glaucon does not want to be "without relishes" (372b), nor does he want to talk about the unsophisticated existence of nonhumans. He does not want to be seen or to live like a pig. However, it is Glaucon's view of what sophisticated human life looks like that ends up quickly terminating in the kind of existence that he is trying to avoid. "There was no need" (373c), Socrates declares, for "swineherds . . . in our earlier city" (373c). There is such a need in Glaucon's. There are, then, actual pigs (and those who enjoy the animals' flesh in abundance) as well as, more metaphorically, Circe's pigs[75] in cities precisely because of

Glaucon's strong resistance to providing for a city that houses the animals. This resistance is part and parcel of the worldview that prevents Glaucon from noticing that the relishes, sophistications, and conventional pleasures for which he calls can dehumanize just as well.

It is not the case that poetry or theater, introduced in book II (373b–c), are intrinsically dehumanizing,[76] and neither are any of the sophistications proposed. It is rather the case that any of them can be depraving and depraved, especially if such arts are considered as completely free from the potential to be corruptive pleasures. The question of the relationship between pleasure and the organization of the polis is at the forefront of the conversations in the *Laws* (636e–637e). In the *Republic*, the sustained discussion of necessary and "unnecessary and useless pleasures" serves as the frame for a presentation of the multifarious and dangerous inclinations of a democratic citizen (558d–561d). Food—a pleasurable necessity—when it is misused serves as an example of degradation in book II. The sense of the reversed relationship between food and its consumption, in Glaucon's luxurious city, is clearer in the Greek, where "*tôn allôn boskêmatôn pampollôn*" (373c) is a metaphor that speaks "of the many fattened fed" creatures and identifies the function of the many as that thing which is being fed.[77] It is, then, as if the many (whether the many human beings or the many beasts) exist for the sake of being stuffed with food in the luxurious city, instead of food being sought out for the sake of sustaining the well-being of the many.

Glaucon understands the sophistication of human beings to be dependent on enjoyment derived from the consumption of goods and services without which, according to him, humans are pig-like.[78] It is this view of the relationship between access to pleasures and sophistication that quickly swells the city with ills. The purification of the fevered, sick, and swollen city (372c–374d) is necessitated by Glaucon's unwillingness to belong to the class of those whom he considers to be unsophisticated or lowly. In the light of this configuration of the dialogical beginning and with an eye on the discrepancy between Glaucon's averred and veiled desires, how are we to interpret the exchanges about the ascent to the Good?

The paradigm that establishes the strict division between what is ugly and what is fair (506c–d), between what is generated and what is "beyond being" (509b), and between darkness and light (508d) can be put to the test of the very same speeches that it structures. This sublime or sublimating paradigm, especially if it is seen in the light of the various references to pleasure, initiates a shift in the meaning of the speeches.[79] Plato sets up a comedic scene that is acted out by two characters—a pleasure enthusiast, Glaucon, and Socrates, who on this occasion plays the didact. The scene, which on my interpretation aligns it with what Hyland understands as a dialogical agon, shows that the sublimation of a desire for pleasure, for instance, is never fully successful at extinguishing that desire.[80]

A pursuit of perfection, no matter how sublime, always aims at a more or less particular look of things. This look itself ends up being telling. It includes the founding desire and what is sublimated in the course of the pursuit of that desire. On this reading, we observe and hold in tension the desire for a kind of exclusive purity or perfection that propels the ascent to the Good, and its grounding impetus, which is Glaucon's ravenous desire for pleasure (ranging from the delights of food and the erotic pleasures of sex to the more *thumatic* pleasures of being esteemed and honored).[81] The comic moments that grow out of this tension situate and animate the dialogical philosophizing (the thinking that probes and pokes fun at the reader's own prejudices, desires, and beliefs) with which Plato's writing is alive. The tension between the desire for pleasure, whether Glaucon's or ours, and the impossibility of the successful purgation or purification of that desire,[82] can only be resolved if we read the dialogue prescriptively; that is, if we take the Kallipolis, the rule of philosopher-kings, and the separation of the city dwellers' classes, for instance, to be Plato's model for an actual city. I steer clear from such an unabashedly literal take on Plato's writing. However, I also argue that it is imprudent to dismiss too quickly all prescriptive readings of the dialogue.[83] For one, such readings have informed political ideas that helped shape some of the most unseemly regimes in history.[84] Also, there is a pedagogical value in grasping the implications of straightforward readings of the *Republic* in order to thereafter dismantle this simplistic take on Plato's thought. Such an approach is valuable because it teaches us about the point of view and the disposition of a person who would prefer to take the dialogical interlocutors at their word. Once we have familiarized ourselves with such a view of the dialogues, we are better positioned to find pedagogical routes that would lead the readers of Plato past the surface meaning of the text. One such device that I rely on here as I make my way through some of the most precarious passages in the *Republic* is—comedy.

In his awareness of the difficulties that have to do with liberating ourselves from a proclivity to take prescriptively or on faith all the dialogical exchanges, Sallis begins his chapter on the *Republic* by issuing a warning. He writes that "to undertake to read the *Republic* carefully and thoughtfully is to place ourselves under the demand for the most severe self-restraint and for the most evocative play."[85] The former is required so that the interpretation does not end up being another reiteration of dogma into which many of the dialogical passages are turned. The latter serves to attune the reader to the self-undermining character built into some of the key arguments and images in the dialogue.

A playful reading, that is, a kind of reading which considers the dialogue as a performance, discerns the dramatic as well as the poetic and mythic elements in it. These elements, in turn, qualify the dialogical exchanges. The enthusiastic ascent in the middle books is taken out of its context if we fail to notice that the "*Republic* begins with *Socrates' descent into Hades.*"[86] Glaucon's felicitous acceptance of the speeches about the Good is misunderstood if these are uprooted from their doubly dark impetus. The reduplication of Glaucon's dim origins, as Benardete explains, has to do with the fact that Glaucon does not quite know what he is talking about. Another indication of Glaucon's negative characteristics is that he is willing to amplify the sentiments of the tyrannically minded Thrasymachus, which means that Glaucon is traversing a psychological darkness or darkness of character.[87] The ascending and the seemingly revelatory speeches recede back into their seemingly obscuring counterparts. Freydberg insists, in his chapter on "Play and Activity of Philosophy," that both tragic and comic elements make up the literary structure of the dialogues and cannot be excised from Plato's writing without doing damage to the meaning we can glean from these extraordinary texts.[88] I seek to identify the so-often-missed destructive potential with which even, or perhaps especially, the most exalted dialogical exchanges are alive. In so doing, I take Plato's comedy, and especially his echoes of Aristophanic plays, seriously.

I analyze Plato's engagement with comedy as a genre. More specifically, I bring to the fore the language, imagery, and scenes in the *Republic* that bear close proximity to the same literary devices in the plays of Aristophanes—the one comedian who, as this text shows, left an indelible mark on Plato's writing. In chapters 2–4, I analyze books V and VI of the *Republic*, which (with their discussion of the best city and the Good) are often seen as a speculative apex of the text. My analysis destabilizes these up-building readings by putting Plato's *Republic* in dialogue with Aristophanes's *Assembly Women*, *Knights*, and *Birds*.

CHAPTER 2

Communist Terror: *Republic* V and VIII and the *Assembly Women*

Religious Festivals at Athens in Aristophanes and in Plato—Scirophoria, Bendideia, Panathenaea

Aristophanes's *Assembly Women* displays an enactment of the plot that the women conspired to carry out at the festival of Scirophoria. The celebration, which took place in the twelfth month of Scirophorion, marked the end of the year and the rebirth of the earth. This was the time for setting new things into motion and putting old things which had outlived themselves aside. The Scirophoria was marked by license and the loosening of the established order but also, conversely, by solemn hours of fasting. The festival welcomed women to leave their households, gather together, and sacrifice at their husbands' expense. The priestess of Athena as well as priests of Poseidon, Erechtheus, and Helios presided over the sacrifices, which crowned a sacred procession from the Acropolis in Athens to Sciron—a holy site that lay along the way to Eleusis and at which the sanctuaries of Athena, Demeter, and Persephone had stood since archaic times.[1]

Aristophanes's play mirrors the festival's inversion of the customary way of things. The women wearing their husband's tunics which they stole, and sporting fake beards (however they came by those) show up at the assembly and take charge of the government. Women now rule and men stay at home. The religious celebration that was an occasion for women's conspiracy gives rise to a new political order. Religion and politics are thus joined at the hip at the beginning of the *Assembly Women*, just as the two are coupled at the outset of Plato's *Timaeus*, *Parmenides*, and the *Republic*.

These three dialogues set sail under the auspices of celebratory, spectatorship events meant to commemorate Athens's military and political prowess.[2] The *Republic*, unlike the other two dialogues, refers to the newly inaugurated Bendideia festival and not to the much older and more traditional Panathenaea.[3]

The Panathenaic festival traced its origin to the time of Erechtheus, a mythical founder of Athens.[4] The quadrennial festival, with its city-wide worship of Athena, resumed with newfound enthusiasm in 566 B.C.E. under Pisistratus who sought to unite Athens and stoke the citizens' national pride. The Panathenaea under Pisistratus brought both rich and lower-class Athenians together as they participated in athletic competitions, religious worship, and animal sacrifices. In the next century, under Pericles, the Panathenaea revived the glorious memory of the Athenians' victory over the Persians as Athens, meanwhile, wagered it could win the Peloponnesian War.[5]

The Bendideia festival marked the success of the Athenians' strategy to strengthen their hold in Thrace. The history of this strategy exposes Pericles's interest in establishing a maritime empire. The year 447 B.C.E. was decisive for Pericles. First there was a campaign in the Thracian Chersonese. Plutarch thought that this campaign was carried out for the sake of protecting the Greeks who lived there from Thracian attempts at retaking the region (Athenian strong-man presence in Thracian Chersonese dates back to the times of Pisistratus).[6] In the same year, 447 B.C.E., according to Jacob Burckhardt, "Athens was defeated at Coroneia, and lost her influence in Boeotia and the other regions of Central Greece, then Megara deserted, and Euboea, intending to do the same, had to be harshly disciplined by Pericles."[7] These disciplinary actions were not the last in Periclean plans at re-entrenching Athenian dominance. B. X. de Wet draws on the information available in the *Athenian Tribute Lists* in order to establish that by 446 B.C.E. it became clear that "the revolt of Euboia and its suppression was the last manifestation of the old and recurrent tragedy in which the allied cities one by one had found that they were indeed not free, but completely at the mercy of Athens."[8] Relying on this machinery of imperial expansion, Pericles continued to subdue territories and peoples. De Wet describes the details of Athenian aggression in Colchis and Eretria. He writes that "at Chalcis the Hippobatae were expelled and their lands, the richest in Euboia, were confiscated by Athens. At Chalcis and Eretria every adult citizen was forced to take an oath to be loyal to the Athenian democracy, while men and boys were taken as hostages from Chalcis, Eretria, and probably from other cities, and kept for some years in Athens. Military measures were taken to prevent revolt."[9] George W. Cox in a book fittingly named, *The Athenian Empire*, establishes the ways in which colonization secured Delian influence and power. He thinks that "the great aim of Pericles was to strengthen the power of Athens over the whole area of the Confederacy. The establishment of cleruch[ies *sic*] who retained their rights as Athenian citizens, had answered so well, that he resolved to extend it. The islands of Lemnos, Imbros, and Scyros [*sic.*] were thus occupied, and

Pericles himself led a body of such settlers as far as Sinope which became a member of the Athenian alliance."[10] The territorial gains were reinforced and further secured through strengthening cultural ties. Religious festivals were one such fine way to insure cultural cooperation.

The cult and festival of a Thracian goddess, Bendis, were inaugurated at Athens in 430/429 B.C.E. (and shortly after 431 B.C.E., which was a momentous year in the history of the Peloponnesian War).[11] The reason for this religious innovation, as Petra Janouchová tells us, was "closely connected with the alliance between Athens and the Thracian king Sitalkes." Janouchova continues, the "[Athenians] wished to conquer Chalkis and surrounding Thracian lands, eventually getting rid of . . . Thracians [under] . . . the king Sitalkes, who possessed an army of soldiers and riders, well trained for the attack. To win the favour of Sitalkes," we learn further, Athens extended the invitation of guest-friendship to the brother-in-law of the Thracian king and offered citizenship to his son, thus strengthening the ties between Athens and Thrace.[12]

For us, the Bendideia festival marks the political advantages of smartly arranged alliances and of religious innovation. It also serves as evidence of an overly zealous attitude in matters of political security and strength.[13] On my interpretation, the instauration of the festival of Bendis is a case in which Athens's political interests precede her religious ones.[14] Plato's concern with this order of priorities is evident, as it is none other but this new festival of Bendis, which serves as the masthead of Plato's *Republic*.

From the start, the *Republic* displays a somewhat risky interest in innovation. This concern will return at 422a and 424b, where innovation is decried, and then again in a different context, at 561e, where the newfound practices bring about the multifarious (*pantodapos*) democratic regime that conceals great political dangers, but also makes room for the study of philosophy. Democracy is not as new to the Greeks as the communist city founded in speech. However, Plato's dialogical characters in the *Republic* are not the only ones who are experimenting with the communist regime while founding their city. Aristophanes's comedy puts up on stage the perils of utopian equality. In what follows, I argue that Aristophanes's *Assembly Women* offers a playful critique of communist equality. I bring this critique to bear on the proposed innovations in *Republic* V.

Comedy of Innovations in the *Assembly Women* and in the *Republic*

The theme of the old and the new was a recurrent trope in ancient Greek comedy. In the *Assembly Women*, it takes on the guise of the opposition between the customary way of doing things and innovation. There, Praxagora praises the women for their steadfastness and adherence to tradition (221–29). The orthodox character of the women's practices, as Freydberg observes, is exemplified by "the way they die their wool. The dye stays fast and does not fade. By contrast, the men would seek to meddle with some innovation . . . even if the ancient custom functioned very well."[15] The women, Praxagora claims, resist innovation. This is, of course, a funny statement, because what Praxagora seeks to accomplish is one of the most radical innovations of all—women at the helm in Athens; women as the rulers and leaders of the city's political regime. Praxagora's unorthodox plan finds support in the predilections of the Athenian "spectators," who "love novelty as well as quickness [and] detest the old and the slow, i.e., they detest moderation."[16] Aristophanes portrays his audience as being excessively fond of all the things that wash away attachment to established customs, laws, and order. The Athenians of his day are so much in favor of novel notions that at the hands of the comedian, their political commitments and interests amount to a brute rejection of the old regime. Strauss's synopsis of the political framework on which the comedy rests is that the "starting point of the new order is the simple rejection of the equation of the good with the ancient."[17] This rejection leads to another equation that identifies the new with the desirable and the good. Admittedly, on its surface, the *Assembly Women* does not offer reflections on the retrograde and the progressive modes of belief. At its surface, the plot of the play does not unfold along the lines of dialectical analysis. However, this does not disqualify Aristophanes's work from being philosophical. It offers to us the possibility of raising questions that are philosophical in nature, but it does not impose such questioning. As a work of dramatic art, Aristophanes's *Assembly Women* eschews didacticism. It is not prescriptive or dogmatic, but entertaining through and through. In the spirit of such excellent, unassumingly thought-provoking entertainment, I will let the comedy speak to Plato's dialogue and trace out the main lines (the conceptual and aesthetic junctures) of this conversation. Both in the *Republic* and in the *Assembly Women*, the characters seek to legislate and—whether in practice or in speech—to bring into being a new political regime. In the comedy, Praxagora succeeds.

In the *Republic* (books IV–VI), the relationship between politics, innovation, and religiously sanctioned practices exhibits the following arrangement: political motives justify novel practices and ideas, insofar as the end-goal of politics is to unite and embolden the polis. Religious cults and rituals, in their turn, facilitate the acceptance of new political relationships and order (427b), which, once they are installed and take root in the community, will guard against innovation in practices and laws. We see this linking-up of the proposals for a new legal structure of the city-state and the supporting religious sanctions in *Republic* V (459e–460a).

The actions of the dialogical characters (Polemarchus and Adeimantus) at the beginning of the fifth book recall the opening of the *Republic*. There, Polemarchus's slave gets hold of Socrates's cloak, stops him, and bids him to wait for Polemarchus (327a–c). In the first scene of book V, Polemarchus himself reaches for a cloak, but now he snatches Adeimantus's garment and asks him: "Shall we let it go or what shall we do?" (449b). The *Republic* begins by placing physical limitations on the freedom of Socrates's actions. Book V metaphorically mirrors such limits, but now it concerns the movement of Socrates's arguments. The conceptual drift of book V breaks with the discussion of the types of regimes which began at the close of book IV. The interlocutors return to this discussion only at the beginning of book VIII. The change in the subject matter reflects the demands that Polemarchus places on Socrates. These demands circle back to Polemarchus's initial understanding of justice as reciprocity between friends (332a). At the start of book V, Polemarchus stops and redirects the progression of the narrative, as he bids Socrates to tell everyone about the new arrangement of the city in which "women and children, the things of friends will be in common" (449c).

The scholarship on the just arrangement of the city in speech covers such topics as the relationship between justice and upright moral psychology,[18] the supposed flaws in Plato's arguments about justice,[19] developments in feminism,[20] and questions of women's rights.[21] One scholar, stressing the link between psychology and politics, concludes that the "defense of a just life" relies on a "complex developmental psychodynamics of remarkable depth and subtlety."[22] Another commentator claims that book V offers a response to the discussion about just rulers in book I.[23]

Although theories of political moral psychology, feminism, and communism can and have been derived from Plato's dialogues and especially on the basis of the *Republic*, I claim that theoretical approach to Plato's writing is only then holistic and rigorous when theory returns to its theatrical roots. For the ancient Greeks of Plato's time, even after Pythagoras's attempts to cleanse theory of its theatrical and sensual alloys, *theôrein* still issued an invitation to spectate. For contemporary readers of Plato this means that if we wish to give due care to the interpretation of his work, we have to be sensitive to the dialogical appearances of theatrical drama. Since Plato's dialogues, unlike Sophocles's tragedies or Aristophanes's comedies, were not performed at the City or the Lenaean Dionysia and, in all likelihood, were not meant for the stage, this further means that we should aim to detect the dramatic action in Plato's *speeches*.[24] With this goal in mind, I analyze the *dramata* in the *logoi* and the *muthoi* that Plato writes.

Attentiveness to Plato's playfulness in the way that he uses language puts the present analysis in conversation with authors like Strauss (1966), Freydberg (2008), Ellis (2011), and Saxonhouse (1978).[25] The latter notes that the *Republic*'s "language seems to undercut the ostensible perfection of Socrates's city and illustrates rather its connections to the comic world of Aristophanes" (888). In Ellis, who observes that "Aristophanes produced a play depicting his own ideal state with provisions similar to those we find in Plato," I see an affinity to my own interest in political innovation.[26] In agreement with Saxonhouse, I trace out "similarities in the communistic programs, both economic and social, and the introduction of women into the ruling classes" (891). These developments in the comedy and in the dialogue, Saxonhouse claims, "suggest a close link between the two, but the significance of the link has seldom been considered with attention to the attendant comic interrelationships" (891). Following Saxonhouse's interpretation, I take up the question that she asks: "If it is funny in Aristophanes, why isn't it funny in Plato?" (891).[27] The findings of this chapter conclude that unless we see the comedy in the *Republic* and unless we learn to appreciate Plato's jokes, we fail to learn from the *Republic* the art of playfully probing our own most gruesome and most promising political realities and ideals.

One of the most serious themes and, ostensibly, the core concept of the *Republic*—the idea of justice—is itself the subject of a joke. At 427c–d and 435a, Socrates advises Adeimantus to get some good light (*phôs*) in order to find justice, and then justice itself bursts into flame like a fire from the rubbing sticks (*pureiôn eklampsai*). If it is not immediately clear why these lines treat justice in a joking manner, consider the role of fire and light in Aristophanes's play. As a comedy, it portrays more crudely and therefore more apparently the faults of the very same political ideas and psychological attitudes that Plato's dialogue presents in a subtle manner.

In the first lines of the *Assembly Women*, Aristophanes's Praxagora, the innovative business lady of the marketplace, implores her lantern, which she claims "possesses the honor of the sun" (5), to "send a signal" to her friends in arms (6).[28] We learn as the play unfolds that Praxagora and her female comrades conspire to mount a political fight for a better life for the citizens of Athens.[29] In short, the women make good plans to fight for justice.[30] The funny flip side of the lantern scene emerges straight away. The light shines both as a sign for Praxagora's fellow conspirators to hurry on along to the appointed meeting, but also, as Praxagora herself tells us, the lamp shines a light on the erotic escapades and petty thefts of the women. Justice, on this comedic model, goes both ways—it lights up the city with the women's far-reaching plans for political revival, and it also brings into the light the problematic character of our desires, as well as the vices to which some of our desires can give rise. The comedy establishes this double-sided character of justice from the start and remains true to it, because it is very funny to see how the seemingly beautiful and just political arrangements drag in with them all sorts of incongruities and vices old and new. In the *Republic*, by the time we get to the communal life and justice described in book V, much of the concern with vice (let alone with vices particular to the novel political arrangement) is left behind. The multitudinous vices which Socrates mentions at the end of book IV (448c) are only picked up again when the conversation circles back to the dissipation of political regimes in book VIII (545e ff.). There and in book IX, corruption is a great worry.

Sham Equality—The Comedic Revelations and Political Blunders of the "Best Regime"

Book V ostensibly outlines the best regime, which is free from corruption. However, Socrates's introduction of the conditions that must hold in order for the ideal society to flourish are much less confident than Praxagora's presentation of very similar ideas in the *Assembly Women*. Socrates worries, but not because he is afraid of being laughed at as much as he fears coming up short of the truth (451a). One of the ridiculous innovations that has to become the new norm is communal and naked exercises (452a–d). Both men and women, old and young, would have to take part in this practice. Glaucon parries that "it would look ridiculous in the present state of things" (452b). Socrates reassures the young man that, with time, this novelty will cease to seem abrasive, just as the custom of naked exercises among men (which was adopted from the Cretans and the Lacedaemonians) at first served as the subject of comedy, but now is very much a common matter (452c–d). Equality between women and men, which is a requirement for the best and the most just city, extends to the equal treatment of the male and the female body in naked athletic training. Although it seems ridiculous, we are told that this innovation has to be taken seriously (452c).

The *Assembly Women* treats the question of equality in a similar context but takes it one step further. The comedy forgoes naked athletics and goes straight to sex. Praxagora decrees that the customary attitude to sexual relations must be revised. And since her cross-dressing ploy to overcome the male opponents in the assembly is successful, her new decree carries legal power. According to Praxagora's new law, anyone can have sex with anyone else, but on this one condition—that the young and the most beautiful ones first satisfy the lecherous desires of the very ugly and the old (611–34). This stipulation goes for both males and females. Aristophanes shows the funny as well as the problematic side of such a lawful mixing. Neither the young women nor the young men are in the least interested in abiding by such a funny legal prescription, since the law serves the ugly and the old. In the *Republic*, this implication of communal nakedness is tamed down, but Aristophanes's comedy shines the light on its political conclusion. The law—both in the *Assembly Women* and in the *Republic*—that seeks to establish a communal disinterestedness in matters of erotics (in the comedy) and of the physical state of the body (in the *Republic*) cannot possibly reach its aim. There is an inner contradiction that is built into the proposed law. This contradiction prevents the law from bringing about the very state of affairs that it legislates. If the citizens happen to be law-abiding (*Assembly Women*) or are taught to be law-abiding (*Republic*), then at least some of them—the young and the beautiful—will get not an equal share of the pie of physical delight and erotic pleasure, but the short end of the stick. Thus, the law that seeks to install absolute equality is incapable of serving everyone equally well.

The lottery of marriages (459c–460a), which the new regime regulates in the *Republic*, elicits Glaucon's concern with the establishment of parental relations (461c–d). Specifically, Glaucon is worried that the city, which has all children in common and goes out of its way to conceal the identity of their biological familial ties, will fester with incest. Glaucon asks: "How will they distinguish one another's fathers and daughters?" (461d). Socrates gives a mathematically driven response about seasonal mating (460d–e) which hardly guarantees that incest is ruled out. Praxagora has to answer a very similar question posed to her by her husband, Blepyrus, who queries: "But if we live this way, then how will it be possible for us to know one another's children?" (635). Praxagora's reply is unambiguous and straightforward. She states, "the old ones will be considered as fathers to everyone. With time this will become customary practice" (637–38). Blepyrus does not cry out against the clear legalization of incest. Instead, he worries that the young men, untethered from familial ties, will take up with a newfound zeal the old and ugly habit of father-beating; which is to say, the habit of beating up anyone older and weaker than themselves. However, a young woman, later in the play, expresses her disgust with the unsavory mixing of ages and genders. She says indignantly that "it is not prudent" (*ou sôphronousa*, 1039) for the young lads to lie with women who are old enough to be their mothers (1039–40). She sharply notes that if such laws are set and if they take hold, then "the whole land will be filled with Oedipuses" (1040–41). In the

Republic, Glaucon's rightful questioning of a regime where fathers might slip into bed with their daughters is all too quickly and unconvincingly abated. The *Assembly Women* does not hide the gross aftermath of communal family and free love—mothers, knowingly or not, are likely to end up having sex with their sons. Presumably, similar problems obtain for homosexual relationships, but these forgo the question of procreation. Thus, Plato paints in hushed colors what Aristophanes puts on display.

The politicization and legal regulation of sex, which are aimed at turning the whole of the city into one big family—whether thriftily run by economical women in the comedy (598–600) or woven into a unitary whole through communally shared pleasures and pains in the *Republic* (462b)—may look like a beautiful idea in theory, but it is unseemly and perverse once it is put into practice. We can laugh off these untoward developments and try to save some of the political and social suggestions outlined in book V. However, that would not be the same as putting ourselves—our predilection for certain kinds of idealism in politics, for example—into the place of the subjects of Plato's comedy.[31] It is advisable to carry out such a substitution because through political and philosophical comedy, we stand to learn about the dangerous and ugly underbelly of our own seemingly brightest and best thoughts.

In the *Republic*, these innovative ways of understanding justice and of securing the best regime for a state are a subject of comedy, despite Socrates's exhortations to the contrary. In the *Assembly Women*, the comedic chorus reassures Praxagora that innovations alone are able to please the Athenians (580). The reason for the desensitized state in which Aristophanes finds Athens tracks closely the taste for innovations of a democratic man in Plato's *Republic*. The dialogue puts tyranny with all of its aberrant passions immediately after democratic splendor, where the old customs give way to everything that is entertaining, iconoclastic, and new. The comedy makes it apparent that Praxagora's communist regime, much like democracy in the *Republic*, gives rise to desires that rear such characters as Oedipus, the tyrant. Both Aristophanes and Plato draw our attention to predatory politics in the aftermath of the Peloponnesian War. Despite the Delian losses, not everyone in Athens sided with the Spartan contingent in their efforts to curb hegemonic moods. The imperialistically minded Theban faction (formed in 404 B.C.E. by Athenian refugees in Thebes) sought to revive Athens's imperialist spirit after it had lost the war. As Laude Mossé contends, the instigators hoped that Athens would benefit from the growing animosity between Sparta and Thebes. They gathered supporters to defeat the Spartans, who opposed the idea of pursuing further expansion and predation.[32]

I now examine the communal and the democratic city as the two obverse sides of the same political arrangement that serves as a fertile ground for tyranny. William Casement holds that both democracy and communism in the *Assembly Women* are subject not only to ridicule but also to Aristophanes's critique. He understands the "unifying political message of the play to be that democracy and communism are bound to fail, as both derive from the same infirm root—the principle of equality. In fact, communism may be seen as a grotesque extension of democracy."[33] I apply Casement's analysis to the *Republic*, where already in book V Plato presents us with an image not of the wholly beautiful and just, but of a very problematic and, if not ugly, then at least a "laughable" city.[34] Although there are important structural differences between the regime described in book V and the democratic polis of book VIII, both are concerned with equality. One of the reasons why democracy in the *Republic* devolves into a tyrannical regime has to do with the relationship between equality and freedom. The attitude that democratic people have toward freedom dictates a leveling-out of all activities and desires in respect to their worth. In a democracy, genuine freedom which abides by the limitations of human nature gives way to a phantom freedom. Fantastical or "insatiable" (*aplêstia*, 562c) freedom, as Socrates calls it, cannot be attained. However, the many fruitless desires that drive human beings to demand such limitless freedom persist and flourish in a democratic state (561a–c).

Aristophanes showcases what Socrates means by "pleasures belonging to . . . bad desires" (561c) at the end of his play, when two old women attempt to satisfy their pleasure-seeking desire to have sex with a young man (877–1163). It is not problematic in its own right that human beings desire sex. However, the fact that Praxagora's new law makes it illegal for the young to deny sexual favors to the old is very troublesome. In Aristophanes's play, the old and the young have to abide by the law that seeks to level out natural differences. This is a sham equality. A case in point: although, in our society today and in principle, younger people are free to have sex with the older, in practice, this does not happen often (at least as far as the non-transactional sexual relations are concerned). In the democracy of book VIII, to follow the same example, all pleasures (and we assume sexual pleasures as well) are equally worthy of satisfaction, regardless of how appropriate or wholesome they are. The theoretical underpinning—the democratic principle of equality, which drives the devolution of this regime—is legalized in the *Assembly Women*. The principle of communist equality is held up as an example of the best city in the *Republic*. However, the best city fails. This failure, in the *Republic*, is not due to the outcomes of the complicated calculus of seasonal birth (546a–547a), but because the principle of equality on which it relies cannot be soundly brought into practice.[35]

The communist ideal that subsumes the individual under the common good and identifies freedom with equality engenders a state that breeds a great disinterestedness in any but self-directed and selfish activities. Thus, the communist ideal contains its own antidote and a principle of its own destruction. The *Assembly Women* brilliantly stages this in the banter between the two men, one of whom is ready to give up his fair share, while the other denies the prudence of contributing to the commonwealth and claims that he can cheat his way into partaking of communal pleasures without paying his due (746–790). Also in the concluding scene, every participant in the inopportune sexual escapade seeks to satisfy her or his own desire. The law that equalizes everyone's work and effort as well as everyone's right to the pleasures of life is untrue to the variegated nature of life. It opposes its own idea in the enactment thereof.

Democracy, which looks much different from communism, nonetheless engenders the same interest in self-aggrandizement and self-gratification. If all activities and desires are of equal worth and all citizens are equally free with respect to their choice of lifestyles, then what remains as the basis for differentiation? It is all too often the sheer force of the assertion that *my* choice is the right one, *my* rights have to be honored, *my* work is meaningful, and *my* desires are the ones that deserve to be satisfied. In other words, it is nothing in addition to or besides the freedom granted to *me*—"I" am the locus of difference. However, the view that the individual is the site of privileged demands placed on freedom runs counter to the democratic ideal of freedom understood as an equal and a common right. In this—the commonly shared kernel of the self-centered and self-serving individualism that grows strong precisely in the two regimes which, at least in recent history, make laws designed to breed it out—democracy and communism find closure. They are two sides of the same coin that pave the way to unchecked and, as Socrates says, "limitless" desires. Democracy and communism pay the price for these by devolving into the only regime that flaunts a promise of their satisfaction, that is, tyranny. Plato in the *Republic* spells out the aftermath of falling prey to this tantalizing promise. At the outset of the discussion of the tyranny into which a democratic regime devolves, Socrates singles out the "insatiable desire" (562b–c) for freedom as the main cause of the dissolution of the democratic state and as the cause of its final transformation into tyranny. It is significant that the assessment of desire, which Socrates carries out, determines it as being insatiable. This desire which Socrates has in mind cannot be satisfied. Therefore, the allure of tyranny, which promises to satiate it, is a mirage that threatens to become a nightmare.

In a democratic state, the limitless desire is still coupled with freedom. In tyranny desire is going to run rampant. Tyrannical eros will be utterly unhinged. However, the key point is that the initial destabilization and the utter liberation of desire take place already in democracy. The upshot of this limitless, insatiable desire for freedom is that the citizens completely disregard the limitations imposed upon them by law. Socrates concludes about the near-anarchical inclination of the people in democracy that "if someone proposes anything that smacks in any way of slavery, they [the citizens] are irritated and can't stand it. . . . And they end up . . . by paying no attention to the laws, written or unwritten, in order that they may avoid having any master at all" (563c–e). Democratic equality that promises a guarantee of freedom to each citizen denies the possibility of freedom to any. Socrates's point goes something like this: if I act upon my idea of what I think I should be free to do—regardless of the law—my action will necessarily impinge upon someone else's freedom. Therefore, we cannot all pursue our own ends which are uncharted by any sense of what is lawful and still be equal in democracy. Someone is going to lose in this game that holds a promise of equality, while also guaranteeing freedom (including freedom *from* law) for all.

The principle of equality that the interlocutors lay out in book V is one of the requirements in a democratic regime. The other one is freedom. However, once we get to the discussion of democracy, we see what this free-roaming equality looks like. Socrates describes the equalization and even a reversal of the roles between parents and children, teachers and students, and human beings and animals (562e–563c). The point that Socrates is making stresses the erasure of authority—of the due respect owed to a figure who is authoritative not merely by might or on a whim, but because of her or his experience, expertise, and capacity to take care of others. This destabilization of the relationships between those who have the know-how and those who still must learn and be educated in the ways of family and public life fuels the reactive sensitivity of the democratic character toward any infringements upon her demands for freedom. Without a compass of substantial authority, and given the craving for freedom to disregard all limitations, including the limitations of the law, the democratic individual of the city in speech in the *Republic* is prepared to fall for the empty promises of a tyrant.

In the *Republic*, communist equality is separated off from tyranny by the elitist rule of the philosopher-kings (book VI); by the accounts of the metaphysical underpinnings of their rule (book VI); and also by the discussion of the prospective rulers' education (books VI–VII). Once the construction of the best city in speech is finally accomplished (543c), the conversation enters another *katabasis* and turns to the question of how regimes dissipate. The final and the worst regime that the interlocutors discuss is tyranny. Therefore, between the communist utopia of book V and the accounts of tyranny and the tyrant in books VIII–IX towers the ascent to the Good, as well as the rule and the education of the philosopher-kings. I follow this development in the *Republic* closely. In the next chapter, I lay bare the causes and the ground of tyranny in relation to education in a democratic state (a state represented through two images of democratic rule—one from *Republic* VI and another one from Aristophanes's *Knights*). In chapter 4, I analyze the rule of the philosopher-kings as well as its metaphysical foundations and explain what it has to do with tyranny by putting the *Republic* in conversation with the *Birds*. Throughout my arguments in the consequent chapters, I hold on to the idea that the democratic principle of equality and the promise of great freedom in democracy stand in direct relationship to tyranny. This relationship is true to life. It is both a historical relationship and a connection that Plato's and Aristophanes's works trace out at length.

CHAPTER 3

The Rule of Satiated Mediocrity: *Republic* VI and the *Knights*

From One as the Many to the Many as One

I showed in my analysis that *Republic* V and the *Assembly Women* offer political arrangements that seek to promote an unrealistic equality and give rise to the citizens' desire to distinguish themselves at all costs. *Republic* VI delivers on this desire by elevating the select few to the supreme status of philosopher-kings. In this chapter I will examine Aristophanes's *Knights*, which offers a playful critique of the desire to be and to have more than the rest in a democratic regime. The *Knights* plays up the importance of holding the people in a democracy accountable for the corrupt and avaricious ambition of their leaders. Socrates, in *Republic* VI, places the blame for the misfortunes of the demos upon the unprincipled sophists. However, I will argue that the city in speech implies the same criticism of the many that is explicit in Aristophanes's comedy.

The preferential treatment of the collective at the expense of the individual does not dissolve individuality, but rather serves as a fertile ground for the growth of a self-centered and self-important personality. The communist ideal does not prevent but rather fosters tyranny. The dissolution of the one into the many, which is the philosophical principle that drives the political ideal in *Republic* V, is the flip side of another amalgam whereby the many become one; the public dissolves fully into a single, private being. The elevation of the outstanding individual above the public life of the mediocrity is the philosophical idea that underlies the political arrangements described in *Republic* VI. Therefore, the *Knights*, where loudmouths banter on their way to the top, is the Aristophanic counterpart to the *Assembly Women*—the play in which a communist ideal rules under the watchful eye of Praxagora, a housewife turned business lady. In the *Knights*, the many citizens—the public—turn into a private man, Demos. Somewhat surprisingly, the nondescript, lowborn sausage seller turns out to possess the natural talent necessary to serve Demos. The sausage seller uses his exceptional talents to ascend to a position of power and manage affairs in Demos's house as he sees fit. "The fundamental political predicament," according to Strauss, "is disposed of in the *Knights* by the absorption of the individuals into the individual called Demos, as well as by the absence of women (and children). Aristophanes will experiment with the diametrically opposed solution in the *Assembly Women*."[1] The latter play came out after Athens had lost the war, in about 392 B.C.E. The *Knights* "was produced at the Lenaea of 424, placing first. [It was] . . . the first play that Aristophanes produced in his own name. (cf. 512—45)"[2] With Aristophanes, then, we have a play about sophistry and political corruption (*Knights*) coming first and a comedy about the perils of communist equality (*Assembly Women*) coming out three decades later. In the *Republic* this order is reversed: we first have the utopian community where everything is held in common, and then we have Plato's metaphor for political corruption in the famous image of the ship of state (488a–d). Following Plato, I assume the order that reverses Aristophanes's production of the two plays and consider the *Knights* after the *Assembly Women*. The context of the political regimes that Socrates advocates in books V and VI calls for the reversal of the Aristophanic order of presentation. In the next section, I outline the setup of the *Knights*, discuss the possible historical identities of its main characters, and indicate the conceptual arc of its themes as relevant to political philosophy. Thereafter, I offer a comparative analysis of the criticisms that both Plato and Aristophanes offer on the subject of demagoguery, political brinkmanship, and the pitfalls of democratic rule.

The Dramatis Personae and Action of the *Knights*

In the *Knights* (424 B.C.E.), Aristophanes "made good his promise at the previous year's Lenaea to 'cut Cleon up into shoeleather for the Knights' (*Acharnians* 299–302), even though Cleon in the meantime had become more powerful than ever."[3] Cleon enjoyed this power in Athens when Spartan envoys, in the aftermath of the 425 Pylos affair, offered Athens terms of peace and friendship from which "advantages [were] . . . likely to follow [because] . . . when Attica and Sparta are in concord, the rest of Hellas, . . . will remain in respectful inferiority before its heads."[4] Instead of taking the Spartans up on their offer, "Cleon, son of Cleaenetus, a popular leader at the time and very powerful with the multitude"[5] rallied against the truce. The Athenians sent the Spartan delegation back with nothing. The hostilities at Pylos went on as Cleon took over "Nicias' authority over the Pylos campaign."[6] Cleon delivered to the Athenians not only the warmongering speech, but also an impression that his leadership could make Athens great. Aristophanes did not agree. He saw the avarice and violence of Cleon, the ineptitude of the "other popular politicians who had succeeded Pericles upon his death in 429, and . . . the complacency of the demos" as the ingredients for the demise of the Athenian polis.[7] Cleon was one of the men who "rose to prominence on merit and by giving well-received," albeit not necessarily well-mannered, "speeches in the *ecclesia*, . . . the son of a wealthy leather merchant and tanner . . . [h]e was a pushy, able, and lucky political improviser."[8] Aristophanes's portrait of Cleon leaves for us an image of a vile, politicking shyster, the sort that would most certainly be successful at making his way into a position of power, the place at the helm of Plato's ship of state, only to run it aground.[9]

In the opening lines of the play, it is not Cleon,[10] but the "damn new-bought Paphlagon" (2) who is causing the two other slaves of Demos great distresses. The "barbaric tanner from Paphlagonia" is Aristophanes's stand-in for Cleon.[11] According to the two slaves, the Paphlagonian enjoys his favor with their master, Demos, the owner of the house of Athens, on the basis of "stolen . . . credit from the real generals" who delivered the Athenian victory in the Pylos campaign.[12] "One of the two slaves in the prologue of the play . . . may have been the impersonation of Nicias (358)" with the other one possibly being an artistic rendition of Demosthenes.[13] In this case, Aristophanes presents the Paphlagonian slave—historical Cleon—as having outwitted and outperformed the historical Nicias and Demosthenes at least in the arena of political machination. We can divorce ourselves from the idea that there is a one-for-one match between the identities of the Athenian generals (Nicias and Demosthenes) and Aristophanes's slaves of Demos. Instead, we can suppose that the comedic characters reflect both the individualities of the two leaders and (extending beyond these particular individualities) the characters also represent, express, and comment on a recognizable human type.

The unmistakable characteristic that Aristophanes stresses for the audience of his play is the servility and the pitiable state of the two dramatis personae that greet us in the prologue of the *Knights*. If we take these two to be reflections of generalship, we get a curious and a seemingly oxymoronic situation in which the actors play slave-generals or servile leaders. We have a case in which infirmity and sycophancy are joined at the hip with power, prowess, and authority. "Throughout the scene the characters of the two slave-generals are sharply contrasted. Demosthenes is a bluff, hearty, loud-spoken, heavy-drinking, fighting-man's general, while Nikias is reserved, timid, cautious, pious, ascetic and indirect, a gentleman's general."[14] The two are united in their grief over the harsh treatment they get from their master on account of the latter giving his preference to a cruel, violent new slave.

The wine-loving first slave gives us a rundown on the appearance and habits of the master, Demos, as well as on the situation in Demos's house at Athens. The master has a "farmer's temperament, a bean chewer, [he is] prickly in the extreme, known as Mr. Demos of Pnyx Hill, a cranky, half-deaf little codger." The slave goes on: "Last market day he bought a slave, Paphlagon, a tanner, an arch-criminal, and a slanderer. He sized up the old man's character, this rawhide Paphlagon did, so he crouched before the master and started flattering and fawning and toadying and swindling him with odd tidbits of waste leather" (45–50). And then the slave relates to us examples of Paphlagon's currying favor with the master: " 'Mr. Demos, do have your bath as soon as you've tried only one case.'—'Here's something to nibble, wolf down, savor: a three-obol piece.'—'Shall I serve you a snack?' " (50–55). We know that Paphlagon's fawning words match his unprincipled actions, because the slave complains that "then Paphlagon swipes whatever any of the rest of us has prepared and presents it to the master. Why, just the other day I whipped up a Spartan cake at Pylos, and by some very dirty trick he outmaneuvered me, snatched the cake, and served it up himself—the one I'd whipped up!" (55–58). The wine-loving slave's complaints continue: "He shuts us out and won't allow anyone else to court the master; no, when the master's having supper, he stands by with a leather swatter and bats away the politicians" (59–62). The final accusations against the mercenary newcomer state that "he chants oracles; the old man's crazy about sibyls. And since he sees that the master's a mooncalf, he's devised an artful technique: he tells outright lies about the household staff; then we get whippings, and Paphlagon chases after the servants, shaking us down, shaking us up, demanding bribes, making threats" (63–66).

The master of Athens, Demos, gets sweet-talked and swindled although he should be running the affairs of the house. Although the other slaves are faring poorly, we doubt from this account that their way of serving Demos is any more honest than Paphlagon's, who gives little to Demos. He provides only a slight raise in the jury duty payments or a shorter time at court, but nevertheless gains considerable power over the master. Paphlagon's sweet talk and swindling place him in control at the House of Athens. Being in this privileged position and having the power that comes with it means a lot.[15] The Paphlagonian slave continues to amass his power through knavery, threats, and acts of violence against the other slaves. Note that Paphlagon seizes the "snack" credit for victory in the Pylos campaign, which would have been served to Demos anyway. The slaves, old and new, try to gain favor by treating Demos of Athens to relishes and dainties, which are likened to territorial expansion and the spoils of war.[16] The slave's complaints about Paphlagon's ability to keep the attention of the master focused on himself tips us off to the following arrangement: the slaves squabble, fight, and otherwise vie for the attention of the master and the boon it brings. Paphlagon's perspicacity in human matters amounts to his capacity to know what tricks and methods work on Demos best and which ones work to Paphlagon's own advantage. The tools of trickery are flattery, small favors that are presented as if they were great ones, dainty foods, and oracular incantations.

The action of the play—it being set into motion—depends on the "cooperation of the two" older slaves in their scheming against Paphlagon.[17] The *desis*—the quickening of the plot—depends on the role played by oracles,[18] since Demos is fond of them. Demos, as the first slave describes him, is rough around the edges, but comes from the sustenance-producing farmers' class. He is irritable and hard of hearing. Demos is quite content in the country, but he is not good at managing the affairs of the house, because this skill requires alacrity of the senses and the mind. Demos, the master, is not an idiot per se, but we might say that he is not very well suited to manage the affairs of the House of Athens. Enter the bought household slaves. But the household slaves have no interest in running the house either. They are interested in managing the master, so to speak, in order to take whatever they see fit from the house and keep it for themselves. This image that opens Aristophanes's *Knights* (long before the eponymous Chorus of the young Athenian noblemen appears) is strikingly critical of Athenian political affairs. It is also strikingly similar to Socrates's criticism of those affairs in book VI of the *Republic*.

I would like to make two observations now, before turning to Plato's text. The first thing to note is that the content, and some of the images, as well as the conceptual implications of the description of Demos's house that Aristophanes gives, find their counterpart in Plato's image of the ship of state. There is a scene in the comedy (537–550) that not only draws on the image of artful sailing, but also mentions the know-how of the rightful steersman (*kubernaô*, 543), and thus dovetails with the end of Socrates's image that represents artful rule of a true pilot (*alêthês kubernêtês*, 488d). The second thing is that in the comedy, the reason why we hear about the way of life in the house of Demos is because the not-so-decent slaves want us to know about the cause of their plight. By contrast, in the *Republic* it is the "most decent" (*epieikestatôn*, 488a) on whose behalf Socrates must make a defense speech (*apologoumenon*, 488a). He makes this speech in response to Adeimantus's worry about the sorry state of those who pursue philosophy (*philosophian*, 488b) in the city. Socrates, then, bids us to "listen to the image," which we know as the ship of state. I wish to pass no preliminary judgment on the view of the *epieikês* in Socrates's metaphor. Instead, I want to shift the somber tenor of book VI of the *Republic* into the comedic, albeit not simply a lighthearted, mode. If it is seen through the lens of Aristophanes's humor, then the status of the decent man in *Republic* VI becomes ambiguous.

The preface to the mention of the *epieikês* is the description of the men "perfected by education and age" (487a) to whom Socrates recommends (and Adeimantus and Glaucon agree) we should turn over the rule of the city. The qualities of the ruler in waiting are such that he is "by nature a rememberer, a good learner, magnificent, charming, and a friend and kinsman [*sungenês*] of truth, justice, courage, and moderation" (487a). This description serves as a prelude to another image—that of a deity, Momus, who fell out of favor with the Olympians for the lively criticism and caustic sarcasm that he directed against the great gods.[19] Momus managed to get banished from Olympus for ridiculing "Zeus, Poseidon, Hephaestus, Athena, and Aphrodite."[20] Zeus and Athena are the divinities associated with justice, courage, and wisdom. Hephaestus (especially with an eye on the *Statesman* myth, 274c–d) can be seen as representing practical wisdom or know-how in the arts. Aphrodite is the one who indicates a certain lack of moderation. Socrates attributes these very qualities—justice, courage, wisdom, and moderation—to the most decent man and the best prospective ruler. This playful treatment of the gods (who invoke the traditional virtues that Socrates mentions) should serve as a clue that a comedic criticism is afoot concerning the straightforward meaning of Socrates's proposition about who should rule.

Shortsighted Demos at the House of Athens and in the Ship of State

This section resumes with my analysis of the image of the ship of state (488a–489d) in the *Republic.* I study this image with an eye on the characteristics of the owner of the ship, that is, the demos, and argue that Plato's demos and Aristophanes's Demos (the owner of the House of Athens in the *Knights*) share much in common. This study sets the basis for my conclusion in this book, which is that in a democracy the people must be held accountable for the conditions that allow corrupt individuals to rise to positions of political power. I now turn to Socrates's rendition of the image of the ship of state, keeping in mind the playful coloration that comedy lends to this passage. "Conceive something of this kind happening either on many ships or one. Though the shipowner surpasses everyone on board in height and strength, he is rather deaf and likewise somewhat shortsighted, and his knowledge of seamanship is pretty much on the same level. The sailors are quarreling with one another about the piloting, each supposing he ought to pilot, although he has never learned the art and can't produce his teacher or prove there was a time when he was learning it. Besides this, they claim it isn't even teachable and are ready to cut to pieces the man who says it is teachable" (488a–b). Moreover, Socrates relates, "they are always crowded around the shipowner himself, begging and doing everything so that he'll turn the rudder over to them. And sometimes, if they fail at persuasion and other men succeed at it, they either kill the others or throw them out of the ship" (488c). The sailors take hold of the shipowner, and "enchaining the noble [*gennaion . . . sympodisantas*] shipowner with mandrake, drink, or something else, they rule the ship [*tês neôs archein*], using what's in it; and drinking and feasting, they sail as such men would be thought likely to sail" (488c). This is not all, for "besides this, they praise and call 'skilled sailor,' 'pilot,' and 'knower of the ship's business' [*nautikon men kalountas kai kubernêtikon kai epistamenon ta kata naun*] the man who is cleverer at figuring out how they will get the rule, either by persuading or by forcing the shipowner, while the man who is not of this sort they blame as useless" (488d).

Here we have a shipowner who is *gennaios,* or as Bloom says, "noble." We must remind ourselves that this sense of nobility or pedigree is also used by Socrates to describe a well-born guardian, who is like a well-bred pup (*gennaiou skulakos,* 375a). This "nobility" implies a sense of decency and pedigree that accords with one's well-born descent, and since the ship of state belongs to the people, we are concerned here with the descent of a shipowner who is the personification of the demos. Their breeding notwithstanding, the shipowner in Socrates's image, and Demos in Aristophanes's play, are both hard of hearing (*hupokôphon*, *Republic* 488b; *Knights* 43) and are not particularly sharp by way of other senses. Nonetheless, both hold in their hands the power to decide the fate of the ship of state and the House of Athens. Neither figure is interested in learning how to wield this power, however. Instead, both of them are all too ready to give the reins of rule over to the loudest flatterers and the toughest crooks. Paphlagon and the other slaves rely on handouts and on food—a metaphor for military conquest and expansion—to win the favors and dull the already weakened senses of their master. The sailors in the *Republic* resort to "mandrake, drink, or something else" (488c) to lull or, if need be, force the shipowner into acquiescence. However, both the slaves and the sailors mean to use those distractions and appeasements in order to avariciously use up the sustenance and wealth of the house and the ship. The demos as the shipowner as well as Demos as the owner of the House of Athens get treated as they well deserve.

If Demos is a country man who would much rather not be bothered with the affairs of the city, then we assume that the shipowner (although Socrates does not give us a comparable description of him) is much the same—stalwart, but dim; not from the nobility, but able-bodied; not well-educated, but raised on a healthy diet of bucolic farm life. Both owners retain their taste for the simple pleasures of a life unspoiled by either well- or ill-intended exertions of the mind. In both cases, this lack of sophistication plays into the hand of cheaters, corrupters, and demagogues of the worst kind. The *Knights* clues us in to examples of the sorts of "clever" things that the sailors in Socrates's narrative might resort to in order to get their way, whether it be by persuasion or by force (488d). The chorus of the knights in the play accuses the Paphlagonian crook, who "deafened our Athens with [his] . . . bellowing" (311), of a "brazenness [which] fills the whole land, the whole assembly, the taxes, the indictments and law courts" (303–305). Furthermore, the Aristophanic chorus tells us that the reason why they are so angry at the Paphlagonian slave is because he has "thrown our whole city into a sea of troubles . . . watching from the rocks like a tuna fisher for shoals of tribute!" (309–312). Cleon, whom the Paphlagonian tanner represents in the comedy, is also a likely candidate for Socrates's ire in the *Republic*. However, the blame does not reside solely with manipulative schemers and no-good politicians. Demos, in the *Knights*, also shares in the destitute state of affairs at the House of Athens. In Aristophanes's play, in Plato's dialogue, and in life it is the demos that enables corruption.

The answer to this "sea of troubles" in the *Republic* is—the philosopher-king. In Aristophanes's play it is—the sausage seller. I next endeavor to show, on the basis of the conceptual and literary analogies between Plato's and Aristophanes's texts, how the philosopher-king and the sausage seller—diametrically opposed though they may seem to be—in fact see to it that their respective cities adopt one and the same kind of rule: tyranny.

Wild Animals, Domestication, and Sacrifice as Metaphors for the Management of the State

Both the shipowner and Demos end up being swindled out of the choicest "foods." Food metaphors, and especially ones having to do with meat consumption (as well as with the sorts of beings that can be consumed or treated as animals, monsters, and beasts), do much of the work in both the comedy and the dialogue.[21] I focus specifically on two images that represent the treatment of animals: (1) livestock, or dumb beasts fit for slaughter, and (2) wild beasts. I treat the latter image first and then, in the following section, I explicate the significance of the former image, in which domestic animals portray a certain state and plight of human beings. I also discuss the characteristic traits of the managers who tend to the animals (both wild and domestic).

The mention of wild animals in book VI comes up after the metaphor of the ship of state in the conversation between Socrates and Adeimantus. The context of the conversation concerns the education of the young and the deleterious effects of sophistry. Since Socrates's metaphor describes the troubles with politics in the city but does not offer a solution to the problem, Adeimantus's question, which solicited Socrates's image, remains. Adeimantus's worry is this: "all those who start out on philosophy . . . who linger in it for a longer time—most become quite queer, not to say completely vicious [*pamponêrous*], while the ones who seem perfectly decent [*epieikestatous*], do nevertheless . . . become useless to the cities" (487d). The image of the ship of state explains why those who study the relationship between the world of nature, the nature of things, and political rule end up being deemed useless (488d). The account of the vicious ensues. In it, Socrates blames the sophists for educating the young in the sorts of things that make them clever but corrupt. We learn about this training that it is administered by "the private wage earners . . . [the] sophists [who educate] . . . in nothing other than these convictions of the many, which they opine when they are gathered together, and he [the sophist] calls this wisdom" (493a). Next, Socrates offers an image of a wild beast and describes the sophists' role in dealing with it. "It is just like the case of a man who learns by heart the angers and desires of a great, strong beast [*thremmatos*] he is rearing" (493a). In an underhanded comment on the highly questionable tactics used in political psychology, Socrates says that what the sophists most want to know is "how it [the beast] should be approached and how taken hold of, when—and as a result of what—it becomes most difficult or most gentle, and, particularly, under what conditions it is accustomed to utter its several sounds, and, in turn, what sorts of sounds uttered by another make it tame and angry" (493b). The sophists obtain this knowledge by "associating and spending time with the beast" (493b). This is an intimate, hands-on kind of relationship which enables the opinion-shapers to gain coveted insights into the mechanisms that allow them to control the crowd.[22] This, Socrates continues, the sophist "calls . . . wisdom and, organizing it as an art, turns to teaching. Knowing nothing in truth about which of these convictions and desires is noble, or base, or good, or evil, or just, or unjust, he applies all these names following the great animal's opinions—calling what delights it good and what vexes it bad" (493b–c). In this description, the demos, or the hard-of-hearing shipowner of the previous metaphor, loses its human characteristics and turns into a "great, strong beast" (493a) in need of taming. Those who manage the affairs of the shipowner in this new setting—the sailors—are analogous to the sophists. Socrates is not offering for our consideration some new city or a new set of rulers and ruled. Instead, the focus shifts from economic power (the question of who has access to the wealth of the ship) to political power (the question of who shapes and influences public opinion). Specifically, the image of the human shipowner changes into the image of a nonhuman beast, when we consider the "many gathered together [as they] sit down in assemblies, courts, theaters, army camps, or any other common meeting of a multitude, and, with a great deal of uproar, blame some of the things said or done, and praise others, both in excess, shouting and clapping" (492b–c). Invoking an image that foreshadows prisoners enchained in a cave, Socrates says that at such gatherings of the many "the rocks and the very place surrounding them echo and redouble the uproar of blame and praise" (492c).[23]

The loud, opinionated multitude turns into an unruly animal. The sophists learn how to enchant it and train it to do their bidding.[24] Amidst the raucous gathering, the sophist stands out as the one who is able to listen to the beast and to learn about its habits and predilections. The animal itself—the publicly engaged demos—becomes less sensitive, less attentive, less sensible, and all the more ready to be treated as a beast. The *Knights* offers a counterpart to this image in Demos, who grows absent-minded and dim-witted at the Pnyx (750–755), the meeting-place of the assembly. However, just as the beast in the *Republic* can be tamed, trained, and manipulated, so too in the comedy, Demos's affections can be swayed. The substance that makes Demos glad is sustenance. It is "barley meal," and "barley cakes . . . and hot meal too" (1104–6). In Demos's opinion, the best treatment is equal to the best food, and whoever treats the master best gets the coveted prize—the "reins of the Pnyx" (1108–09). Plato and Aristophanes agree on this: the people en masse are difficult to educate, but not difficult to manage. When gathered in a public space and asked to make political decisions, the demos loses many of its humane characteristics and makes itself vulnerable to being treated like a craven, infirm codger or a powerful but inhuman beast.[25]

If there are any similarities between our own role in contemporary economy and politics and the role of the demos in ancient Greece, we too are surely subject to Aristophanes's and Plato's criticism. For Plato and for Aristophanes, the joke is true to life. If the demos is insensible and politics is husbandry, then as the slave in the *Knights* points out, "political leadership's no longer a job for a man of education and good character, but for the ignorant and disgusting" (190–193).[26] Socrates is somewhat less obvious in his ire. His complaint is that the beast-taming sophist knows "nothing in truth" (493b–c). By this, I do not mean to say that tending animals requires little know-how, but only that both the comedian and the philosopher agree that there is a disanalogy between animal husbandry and the government of a state. Aristophanes draws on the difference to provoke laughter. I will eventually reflect on similar images of animal tending in Plato's dialogue. I claim that these images are not prescriptive, but only suggestive of the sorts of things that have gone awry and continue to go awry in our public life.[27] But before I establish with any certainty that the desensitized and politically careless people deserve the undeserving ruler that they get, I need to show how both in the *Knights* and in book VI of the *Republic*, the ones who rise to leadership are, in fact, unfit. In order to accomplish this, I will explain the way in which Aristophanes's winner in the contest with Paphlagon, the sausage seller Agoracritus, measures up to both the sophist and to the philosopher-king.

The Undeserving Ruler That the Demos Deserves

The first thing we note about the sausage seller is that he merely stumbles onto the path to power (144–148). Oracular pronouncements, god's will, and an opportune occasion make it so. Chance binds the sausage seller to his fate. And we notice in the *Republic* that Socrates's recipe for the institution of philosophy in the rightful "office of king" (499c) has the exact same ingredients. He calls on "divine inspiration" (499b), but only after telling us that the only way a "city [or] . . . regime will ever become perfect" (499b) is if "necessity chances" to bring it about (*anangkê tis ek tuchês peribalê*, 499b). No doubt, Aristophanes's and Plato's men disagree on the matter of the ruler's education. Socrates has clear pedagogical requirements for the young,[28] while Demos's slave clearly does not think that the educated nobility have any serious chance to rule (179–194). Moreover, at the end of Aristophanes's play, the seemingly ignorant sausage seller proves to be much less inept than we might first think. Strikingly, he ends up being a perfect fit for the role of a ruler.

The oracles, which we know Aristophanes's Demos is very fond of (60–61), predict the sausage seller's rise to power. The counterpart of these oracular pronouncements in the *Republic* are some unspecified enchainments in Socrates's image of the ship of state (488c), as well as the clever sophists in the beast-taming image (493b). The oracle scrolls, which give the two slaves hope that Paphlagon's rule in the house will eventually be overturned, are in the Paphlagonian's possession. The wine-inspired slave (the one, which could be Demosthenes) steals the scrolls and sets out to turn them into a self-fulfilling prophecy when he sees a sausage seller passing by the window of the master's house. We learn the name of this sausage seller, Agoracritus, only much later when Demos invests him with the "stewardship" over himself (1260); that is, over the people of Athens.

Despite his name, which associates him with the public place—the agora—Agoracritus, unlike his rival from Paphlagonia, is a private man. Such a man is happy to mind his own but not the public's business. At first he is so doubtful of his capacity to rule that he gives an impression of being unwilling to take on the affairs of the city. But Agoracritus, the oracle carefully predicts, will supersede several other "sellers." The oracle explicitly says that "first there arises a hemp seller [*stuppeiopôlês*], who will be the first to manage the city's affairs. . . . After him there's another one again, a sheep seller [*probatopôlês*]. . . . To hold power until another champion arises who's more disgusting than he, whereupon he perishes" (129–135). The oracle says that the next in line "is a hide seller [*bursopôlês*], our Paphlagon, a robber, a screamer. . . . So the sheep seller is fated to perish at the hands of a hide seller. . . . There *is* one still to come, with an extraordinary trade [*huperphua technên echôn*]" (135–141). And here we learn that the "man who shall destroy the Paphlagonian is a sausage seller [*allantopôla*]. A sausage seller! Holy Poseidon" (143–144).[29]

We have in the lines of the oracle a clear progression (or a digression if you wish) from someone who deals with and sells plants, to someone who sells an entire animal, to those who make their living and then, curiously, their way into politics, too, by selling variously prepared parts of the dead animal. At least one of the men in this chain of political succession dies at the hands of another: the tanner delivers the sheep seller to his death. The assumption that the oracle makes is that there must be someone even crueler than the atrocious Paphlagon to oust the unprincipled tanner. The sausage seller comes to the rescue. He will succeed in deposing the servile crook Paphlagon, who has amassed too much power. Moreover, the sausage seller has an "extraordinary trade." This phrase should give us pause. There is little to nothing extraordinary about making and selling sausages. The Greek reads "*huperphua technên echôn*" (141)—"having a supernatural or monstrous craft." This is odd. What could be more natural than eating? What could be more natural than making a dime by selling food? The sausage seller is the last one whom the oracle mentions. The first one is a "hemp seller," a fellow who barters vegetative stuff. We go, then, from the seed or vegetable product to the sale of animals—whole and parts. The sale of the sorts of things that animals like sheep feed on gives way to the sale of the animal itself. The sellers in the prophecy rise to the ranks of household managers, or rulers of the House of Athens. They win the affection of Demos. He first accepts the services of such slavish knaves who deal in vegetable feed and fodder, and then Demos gives over the reins of rule to the fellows who profit from the sale of dead flesh. This is Aristophanes's metaphor for the succession of rule and the nature of power plays in Athens.

Let us recall that we already said how Demos in the *Knights* compares to the shipowner in the *Republic*. We also stated that the shipowner is the same as the beast whom the sophists know how to tame and rule. Now, we reinsert the image of the animal from the *Republic* back into Aristophanes's play. We end up with a close alignment between the beast and Demos, whom the sophists and the sellers, respectively, know how to manage and treat in order to subdue their vigilance and use up their substance. The sophists learn the temperament of the beast and know how to soothe it. The sellers—and the agon between the Paphlagonian tanner and the sausage seller shows as much—both know the words and the foods that enchant Demos best. There is one more alignment between the personages in the *Knights* and in the *Republic*. Since the shipowner is also the beast in need of taming and the sailors are sophists, too, the shipowner (the beast) : Demos :: sailors (the sophists) : the sellers. Such an alignment suggests why the sausage seller's trade is *huperphuês*. The sausage seller ends up being more formidable than the tanner because if Demos is also an animal, then the sausage seller takes parts of the ground-up beast, wraps these in the lining of the beast's own stomach, and feeds the beast's meat back to . . . Demos, that is, to the beast itself. If this is what the sausage seller ends up doing, then his trade is monstrous and indeed extraordinary. It is not the intent of the sausage seller to rule violently or to partake in monstrous actions. He does not realize the sinister implications of his craft. However, with an eye on this analysis, *we* ought to. In what follows, I apply this insight about the supernatural character of the sausage seller's trade back to the discussions of rule as shepherding (*Republic*, book I). I consider Glaucon's request for relishes (book II) and establish a connection between dainty foods, expansionist war, and swineherds (book II) in the *Republic*.

Thrasymachus, who appears to Socrates as if he were a "wild beast" (*hôsper therion*, 336b) in book I, speaks at length about rule and justice, which he asserts is the "advantage of the stronger" (338b–e).[30] Thrasymachus also introduces the metaphor of herding as rule (343b–344c). According to him, the "shepherds and the cowherds consider the good of the sheep or cows and fatten them and take care of them, looking to [nothing] . . . other than their masters' good and their own" (343b). The tame, domestic animals live well under the watchful eye of a good shepherd—until, that is, the time comes for animal slaughter. Thrasymachus's provocation echoes throughout Plato's text, and in this echo we hear the caustic criticism that Aristophanes serves up in the *Knights*. The Paphlagonian tanner and the sausage seller move up from their trades to the position of attendants at the House of Demos. They both fit Thrasymachus's description of the ones who see in the good-looking animal the means to their own well-being and advantage. Thrasymachus differentiates between the ruler, the shepherd, and the herd or those who are ruled. Aristophanes shows that the ruler and the ruled—the demos, or the people to whom power rightfully belongs in a democracy—are on the same side. On the other side are the sellers or, following Thrasymachus's description, the shepherds. Those who practice the arts of animal husbandry, slaughter, tanning, butchery, meat-handling, and meat-preparation stand out. In a democracy, Demos is the shipowner, the beast, and the people to whom the state belongs; that is, the demos. The ruler and the ruled turn out to be one and the same. Note that the "demos," at least in *Republic* VI, where so much time is devoted to nobility of character and the benefits of education, does not solely designate a hoi polloi or a democratic rabble. In the *Knights*, too, Demos is from the countryside, but he is not a nobody; he is not penniless. The animal, as Thrasymachus insists, and Aristophanes's jesting threatens, is well-kept, fattened, and fit for slaughter.

In book II, Socrates attempts to redirect the course of the construction of the city and therefore to pivot our understanding of a *politeia*—the city's soul or its regime.[31] This attempt includes excising meat—entirely—from the denizen's' diet (372a–b, 372c–d). Glaucon does not agree. The young aristocrat calls for "relishes" (372c).[32] Socrates half-playfully, half-seriously counters with an offer of boiled onions and such. This will not do for Glaucon, who spitefully claims that such a city, such citizens, and such a diet are only fit for pigs. Socrates understands. We need both dainty foods and meat stuffs; we wish for arts and for courtesans, too; we call for sumptuous banquets, adornments, and fancy couches. A simple city is not enough. Perhaps, it is insufficient because it is not a city at all. Maybe it is not in our nature to make such unadorned living possible. The city that Socrates and Glaucon set out to endow with a regime—and where they seek to discover justice—comes to be because Glaucon will not abide by living like a pig. Plato's dark humor here is that Glaucon's indignation—in the span of several lines—introduces both the said animal and the swineherd into the city. As soon as the swineherd enters the picture (373b), we run into the problem of the dearth of land needed for pasture (373d). To get more land, "we cut off a piece of our neighbors' . . . [we] go to the unlimited acquisition of money, overstepping the boundary of the necessary" (*anangkaiôn*, 373d), which Glaucon affirms happens "quite necessarily" (*pollê ê anangkê*, 373e). The next step is war (373e), and with it the immediate need to divide off a class of warriors, of those who are "fit for guarding the city" (374e). These guardians in the *Republic*, the noble pups (375a), enter the conversation as a class essential for the city which has a well-developed taste for excessive pleasures, including those that come with the accumulation of great wealth. The best city in speech and its classes—purged though they will be—set sail under the auspices of meat consumption and because Glaucon is either unable or unwilling to catch up to Socrates, who latches on to Glaucon's aversion to the simple life and turns this aversion into a sinister joke.[33] Glaucon recoils from living like a pig—from an unsophisticated and, in his eyes, brute existence—only to face a life in the city that offers this alternative: either be herded, fattened, and slaughtered like a pig or treat others like animals fit for slaughter. Aristophanes's Demos, despite all of his sluggishness, understands this (1121–30). The sellers, those who flatter Demos and seek to use up his wealth, resort to the sorts of enticements to win his favor that Glaucon thinks differentiate the good life from a mediocre, swinish existence. Some of the dainty foods and relishes which the Paphlagonian tanner and the sausage seller offer up to Demos are a metaphor for the spoils of war (1005–13, 1166–95, 1214–25). In the *Republic*, we see an analogical alignment between the dependence on the accessibility of certain foodstuffs and the abundance of conquered territories (373b–e).

In the *Republic*, it is less obvious whether the shipowner, who is also a beast in need of taming, is not only an unsuspecting victim of manipulative politicking, but is also himself a perpetrator of cruel and corrupt acts. By contrast, the *Knights* makes it clear that Demos implicates himself in violence and cruel means of managing the affairs of state. The chorus of the knights is unambiguous on the matter when it addresses Demos and remarks on the character and effects of his power: "Demos, you rule so beautifully that all human beings fear you, as if you were a tyrant" (1111–14). This is Aristophanes's serious assessment, although comically presented, of the type of rule that the Athenian demos wields. The knights continue: "You're easily led astray: you enjoy being flattered and thoroughly deceived, and every speechmaker has you gaping. You've a mind, but it's out to lunch" (1115–20). Demos responds, "There's no mind under your long hair, since you consider me stupid; but there's purpose in this foolishness of mine. I relish my daily pap, and I pick one thieving political leader to fatten; I raise him up, and when he's full, I swat him down" (1121–30). In this response, we hear the echo of Thrasymachus's proposition about the nature of rule, which compares the ones who are being ruled to fattened cattle. Demos's retort to the knights' invective is: "I, the tyrannical ruler, only pretend to pay no mind to the conniving, self-indulgent sophists, orators, and public leaders of the day. I let these men have their say, while they serve my needs. I let them think that they hold power over me, but only to confuse them. Once they have taken more from the public funds than I deem to be acceptable, I call the thieves on their corruption and I sacrifice a chosen few, making an example out of them." On Aristophanes's presentation of Athenian politics, it is not so much a single leader who exercises violent—tyrannical—rule over the subjects, but rather it is the Athenian demos itself. The chorus of the *Knights* confirms this conjecture. "In that case you'll do well; and your character really does contain, as you claim, very deep cunning, if you deliberately fatten these men, like public victims, on the Pnyx, and then when you chance to lack dinner, you sacrifice one who's bloated and have yourself a meal" (1131–40). The political hacks seek to disembowel Demos, or at least the House of Athens, and use it for the riches that it holds. Demos, in his turn, sees the corrupt politicians as fattened beasts who can be slaughtered when the need calls for it. This image, where the people are as ready to gobble up the leaders that they place in power, as the leaders are eager to use their power for their own selfish ends, fits both history and Plato's text. I will offer a brief historical excursus next and then return to the *Republic* in order to indicate the conditions that serve as the fertile ground for tyranny in the city in speech.

The Ground for Tyranny

In 425 B.C.E., the sixth year of the Peloponnesian War, the Athenians preferred to follow Cleon's hawkish plan about how to handle matters in the Pylos affair instead of agreeing to a truce with Sparta.[34] The Athenians did not unanimously support Cleon's decision. Nicias "resigned the command against Pylos" and the people "clamored at Cleon to go."[35] However, this was not a show of an all-out support for Cleon, who boasted that "he would within twenty days either bring the Spartans alive, or kill them on the spot. The Athenians could not help laughing at his empty words."[36] We learn that "sensible men comforted themselves with the reflection that they must gain in either circumstance; either they would be rid of Cleon, which they rather hoped, or if disappointed in this expectation, would reduce the Spartans."[37] This was the situation on the eve of the production of Aristophanes's *Knights*. At the time that Plato was composing the *Republic*, the aftermath of the aggressive internal politics to which Aristophanes's comedy draws our attention played itself out.[38] We cannot solely blame the attitudes of unprincipled

Athenian leaders like Cleon, nor can we say that the Athenian demos bore the full weight of the responsibility for Athens's defeat in the Peloponnesian War. Instead, the shortsightedness and self-centeredness of both the people and the politicians gave rise to the conditions that serve as the ground for tyranny in Plato's and in Aristophanes's texts.

On Adeimantus's view, which Socrates tries to meet by recommending that philosophers ought to be rulers in the ideal city, the problem with political corruption is two-pronged. On the one side (and as Socrates explains) there are the selfish "kinsmen and fellow citizens [*hoi te oikeioi kai hoi politai*] [who] . . . surely want to make use of . . . [the young men] . . . for their own affairs" (494b). This is a problem of education. How does a smart young person become good in the city, which by and large is made up of people of questionable moral worth? If the moral compass is not set correctly, then no matter how educated, talented, and intelligent the leader in the wings may be, that young person will not turn out to be good for the city (495a–b). The other side of the issue with political leadership and corruption is that even if someone happens to bypass the unsavory influence of the teachers who know "nothing in truth" (493b–c), in the end that good person "would perish before he has been of any use to the city" (496d). Note that these lines reflect Socrates's restatement of Adeimantus's dilemma (487c–d). Note further that Socrates denies that "we would justly be laughed at" (499b) if we followed his proposed solution of philosopher-kings. The very mention of laughter gives us pause. If Socrates's solution does not hold water, then his mention of laughter implies that we are witnessing not a construction of the best regime and the best city in speech, but the composition of a comedy. Socrates's star-crossed recommendation would have "those few philosophers who aren't vicious, those now called useless . . . take charge of a city, whether they want to or not, and the city [must] . . . obey; or [else] a true erotic passion for true philosophy [must flow] . . . from some divine inspiration into the sons of those who hold power or the office of king, or into the fathers themselves" (499b). Let us recall that the undesirability of the second alternative, which would have the rulers fall in love with philosophy and learn how to philosophize, surfaces later in the dialogue during the discussion of tyranny. In book VIII, we learn that when the tyrant "grows naturally, he sprouts from a root of leadership and from nowhere else" (*hotaper phuêtai tyrannos, ek prostatikês rhitzês kai ouk allelothen ekblastanei*, 565d). Therefore, as great a boon that might chance upon the city in the event that the leader—somehow—becomes passionate about philosophy, the obverse side of the ruler's erotic passion is that sometimes "love in him [grows]—a great winged drone" (*megan kêphêna*, 573e–574a). This love turns the man into a tyrant. I have already indicated the difficulty with the other part of Socrates's requirement, which seeks to establish philosophers as rulers. That difficulty presents itself as the unlikely coincidence between necessity and chance (499b). Let us assume that the event in which "some necessity chances to constrain those few . . . who are not vicious" (499b), positioning them to rule, is exactly what Aristophanes's play portrays. The sausage seller chances to turn up and take charge in the House of Athens according to the necessity of fate that the oracle outlines. And on Socrates's presentation, we must have a philosopher who although useless, takes charge. To make an analogy between Socrates's portrayal of the best ruler and Aristophanes's sausage seller, I now ask: is Agoracritus philosophical, and if yes, then in what way?

Agoracritus is not useless. His trade is in demand. However, it is very difficult to say that he is philosophical. His upbringing precludes him from being a match, according to Socrates's excurses, for the kind of education that philosophical rulers-in-waiting ought to receive. However, there is a certain natural fittingness—a natural talent for winning Demos to his side and running the House of Athens—that Agoracritus exhibits. In his attacks on the Paphlagonian tanner, Agoracritus shows the sort of distanced relationship to his passions that is akin to a philosophical outlook on life. Strauss sees the sausage seller's "natural superiority to Kleon,"[39] whom Strauss takes to be the historical counterpart of Paphlagon, in "the manner in which he responds to his opponent's threats. He is indeed as good as Kleon, or better, at threatening; but while Kleon is genuinely savage and full of hate (as were the knights), . . . the sausage seller only plays the savage; he does not lose his ease and good nature while shouting the terrible things."[40] As far as Agoracritus's agon with and victory over Paphlagon goes, the locus of the sausage seller's emotions and statements is not the sausage seller himself; it is an impersonation of a savvy speech-maker that Agoracritus masterfully enacts. He appeals to the emotions of his audience and gets his opponent riled up. If Aristophanes's play simply ended with the sausage seller's victory and stopped at that, then we could say that Agoracritus is just a natural sophist, or at least a natural orator.[41] Neither of these suffices to make a philosopher-king. However, Agoracritus does not only do what others, such as the tanner, did before him. In addition to banqueting at Demos's expense (1160–1259), Agoracritus aims to reeducate and transform Demos. Note that the sausage seller is initially unwilling to take on the leadership of the state (just like Socrates's best, philosophical man in *Republic* II, 347c). However, once the two slaves take hold of him, Agoracritus abides by their entreaties and demands, which amount to exactly Socrates's worry about "being ruled by a worse man" (347c). Also, if one of the things that Socrates's philosopher-king does is see to it that the city he rules is made stronger (462a–464a), then the sausage seller promises to do just that (1321–30).

Agoracritus claims to bring back the times when the city was renowned for its military might and glory. He revives "Athens the gleaming, the violet-crowned, the envy of all . . . the monarch of Greece and of this land" (1328–30).[42] The return to Athens of old, the resurrection of its former glory, which the sausage seller-made king claims to perform, is the move from dilapidation to political might. *Anarchia* is meant to give way to its opposite, *anarchaidzô*. However, the *Knights* exposes the counterproductive effects of Agoracritus' attempts and shows us that this is not a genuine change but a sham one. Aristophanes peels back the veil of political reform and unmasks its sinister underbelly. Although Agoracritus, at least as far as Demos is concerned, is so fit to rule the House of Athens that it is appropriate to "regard him as a god and treat him accordingly [i.e., as the] . . . absolute ruler of Demos,"[43] the aftermath of Agoracritus's ascent to power is nothing short of tyranny.

The very first thing that Agoracritus does as the man in power is to "boil" Demos down and thus, by means of this purification, transform his "ugliness into beauty" (1321). This is some way to bring about a change in people's dispositions! Whereas Demos was ready to slaughter his slaves if and when they got too greedy—when they were fattened up enough—Agoracritus, who was once the head-slave and is now the head manager (or the ruler) in the House of Athens, "boils" Demos. The individuals who make their way into positions of power, as well as the Athenian demos itself, are ready and willing to use violence against each other. Made youthful, handsome, and glorious by "boiling," Demos is now ready for reeducation. Agoracritus calls for the right measures that are meant to curb corruption (1332–3183), but the moment that Demos agrees to the proposed changes, the new ruler offers Demos a dissipated treat of his own. Agoracritus's actions undermine his speeches. At first, he talks of the restored, good, and rejuvenated Athens and its order. He calls out political machinations and Demos's former weak-willed ways. However, immediately thereafter, he offers up to Demos (to this lecherous creature who does not shun cruelty) three winsome youths—a boy for him to use as a "split-bottom chair" should Demos "get the urge" to do so (1384–86), and two beautiful girls[44] who personify "thirty-year peace treaties" (1388–89). Agoracritus does not reject Demos's request to "lay them down and ratify them" (1391–92). Instead of stamping out corruption, Agoracritus acts like the "dread enchanters and tyrant-makers" (*Republic* 572e) who, if they do not unleash the "unnecessary and useless pleasures" (561a) of a future tyrant, at least encourage such pleasures and pander to the tyrant in the making. We are left with two conclusions. We either face a merely seeming change of order from lawlessness and corruption to the glorious former state—a time when Athens was great—or Aristophanes suggests that Athens was never great and that its corruption is ineradicable.

The godlike figure of the new ruler, who was chosen by a fated chance, is a natural fit for the ruling post in Athens. However, this is not because Agoracritus is extraordinarily smart or because he possesses unquestionable moral mettle. He is neither a philosophical nor a natural-born ruler, and insofar as he is not, there is no direct correspondence between the philosopher-king of the *Republic* and the sausage seller of Aristophanes's comedy. However, Agoracritus is a natural fit for the tyrannically minded Demos. He is the perfect ruler for the kind of people that make up the Athens of Aristophanes's time. This perfect ruler is a tyrant. Agoracritus's actions are metaphors that mirror the descriptions that Plato gives to the tyrannical ruler in *Republic* VIII. Unlike the tyrant in the *Republic*, however, Agoracritus does not proclaim to "be stirring up war" (567a). On the contrary, he offers Demos peace. But Agoracritus's services to Demos aim to please and subdue his master rather than strengthen and improve the House of Athens. As his speeches seem to profess, these services recall the sorts of actions that Socrates characterizes as those of a tyrant. The tyrant, for example, promises "much in private and public, and [promises to] grant freedom from debts and . . . [pretends] to be gracious and gentle to all" (566e), but does not necessarily deliver on these promises. Aristophanes's sausage seller does not have to pretend. He is good-natured. This might be an added twist to Aristophanes's already dark humor—a tyrant of the Athenian demos need not be vicious and perverse. In fact, he could be a rather simple-natured fellow. The rather mild "punishment" that Agoracritus administers to Paphlagon proves as much (1397–1401). However, the new ruler in the House of Demos is tyrannical in his actions toward Demos. The purification of Demos that Agoracritus performs and which includes reducing Demos by "boiling" (*aphepsêsas*) sounds an awful lot like Socrates's supposition that if a tyrant "suspects certain men of having free thoughts and not putting up with his ruling," he will find a pretext "for destroying them" (567a). The tyrant thereby reduces the demos to a preferred, more manageable—call it rejuvenated—size. This sort of size reduction, incidentally, is one of the things that Aristophanes's Lysistrata recommends in her initial, violent solution to the pestilence of the Peloponnesian War. In Plato's and Aristophanes's times, but also closer to the historical moment that is our own, these very measures have been applied time and again to the management of the state.

Plato and Aristophanes agree that the distance between democracy and tyranny (at least in Greece in the fourth century B.C.E.) does not take much effort to traverse. In fact, in the *Knights* it looks as if this distance is all but nonexistent. The people are tyrannical, and those who take the power at the helm are violent, unprincipled, and tyrannical, too. An unwholesome harmony establishes itself between the ruler and the ruled. The seediness and dissipation of the many helps the ones who will continue to corrupt the public to ascend to the top. The comedy suggests that Socrates's proposal will not do. Even *if* someone with a philosophical nature, as Socrates describes it, grows up in the unphilosophical city and makes his way to power, he will not be the natural or the closest fit for those who are in need of being ruled. On the contrary, the mismatch between the leader and those led will have the ruler pinned against a tyrannically minded mass. Thus, it looks as if not the rulers, but the ruled—contrary to Socrates's dismissal of this idea—must learn to think and to be philosophical. The reason that Socrates gives for his claim that "it is impossible . . . that a multitude be philosophic" is that the many are unable to "accept or believe the fair itself, rather than the many fair things, or that anything itself, *is*, rather than the many particular things" (493e–494a). But what if this is not a good reason? What if it is, instead, the claim to intellectual elitism—to knowing and having exclusive access to the idea of the Good itself—on the part of the few that constitutes one of the obstacles to a thoughtful life, to good education, and to the philosophical training of the many? I seek to give an answer to these questions in the next chapter. For now, I conclude by offering a convergent interpretation of Aristophanes's and Socrates's responses to the troubles of Athenian politics.

The Skillful Navigator in the *Republic* and the *Knights*—A Promise of an Artful Life

As I mentioned at the outset of my investigation of the affinities between the *Knights* and *Republic* VI, the image of the ship of state finds two correspondences in Aristophanes's comedy. One of them, discussed at length in this chapter, has to do with the machinations of the no-good leaders and the effects thereof. Another similarity bears on the question of art.

In the *Republic*, we are concerned with the art (*technê*) of the "true pilot" (*alêthinou kubernêtou*), which is the art of politics (488d–489a). In the *Knights*, Aristophanes tells us about his own art, which is "producing comedies [–] . . . the hardest of all tasks" (517–518). The craft in question differs. However, I propose that Aristophanes is as good at exposing political corruption as Plato is excellent at the comedic art. The image that the two authors use to describe the art of politics (Plato) and artful writing (Aristophanes) is—almost one for one—the same. It has to do with sailing. In this section I will offer side-by-side quotations from *Republic* VI and from the *Knights*, and then I will reflect on the striking resonances between Plato's and Aristophanes's images of masterly art and life.

Plato's dialogue says that those who are poor at understanding what political art entails

> don't know that for the true pilot [*kubernêtou*] it is necessary to pay careful attention to the year, seasons, heaven, stars, winds, and everything that's proper to the art, if he is really going to acquire the art and practice of how one can get hold of the helm whether the others wish it or not, and at the same time acquire the pilot's skill. So with such things happening on ships, don't you believe that the true pilot will really be called a stargazer, a prater, and useless . . . by those who sail on ships run like this? (488d–489a)

In the *Knights*, Aristophanes also presents for us an image of sailing. The comic Chorus Leader explains that although "our poet [Aristophanes] . . . hates the same people we do, and dares to say what's right, and nobly strides forth against typhoon and whirlwind" (518–511), there is a reason why he "waited so long to apply for a chorus in his own name" (514–515).[45] The Chorus Leader reminds the audience that their tastes are fickle and that even the celebrated comedians must suffer "violent rebuffs" and this is why "in dread of these precedents that our poet kept delaying" (540–541). Aristophanes was delaying, as Niall W. Slater writes, to present "a play in his own name"[46] or to insert himself in the chorus (for example, as the leading cloud in the *Clouds*).

> And in addition, [our poet] . . . held that one should be an oarsman before handling the tiller, and from there take charge of the bow and watch the weather, and only then become a pilot in one's own right [*kubernan auton heautô*] . . . So for all these reasons, he acted discreetly, and didn't leap mindlessly in and spout rubbish . . . [So let's] raise a big wave of applause for him, and give him an eleven-oar cheer worthy of the Lenaea, that our poet may go away happy and successful, gleaming to the top of his shining head! (515–550)

Both Plato and Aristophanes indicate that the one who wields the art, be it a political leader or a playwright, must know the ins and outs of their craft in order to be worthy of the name. However, what Socrates dismisses, namely the capacity of the many to philosophize, and thus to be able to judge the fitness of a leader (494a), both Aristophanes's comedy and Plato's dialogue acknowledge when they are taken as literary works and works of art. That is, if we leave Socrates's incredulous attitude aside for a moment, we can consider the *Republic* as a piece of literary philosophizing that shows dramatic quality on a par with the most celebrated tragedies and comedies of Plato's time (and ours). If we do this, then we do not listen solely to Socrates's arguments about education, but also watch the action of the dialogue and seek to be educated by it. Just as Aristophanes's comedy challenges us, the audience, whether now or millennia ago, not to be like Demos but to be capable of being educated, so also the *Republic* holds out a hope that we not raise up any single character to the status of a revered and paradigmatic leader, but that we take the dialogue to be a holistic work of art. In this case, we would allow ourselves to learn from the mismatched moments, from the incongruous, if not impossible suggestions made in the dialogue, just as much as we would learn from the arguments that are plausible, the propositions that look attractive, and the exchanges that make—to us now—good sense. We would learn to navigate—as pilots do—Aristophanes's and Plato's texts, and then we would learn from them not as if from a set of prescriptions, not as if they were criticisms of a single system of rule, not as if they presented us with sets of dogmas; but in a *way* laid out by the thinker's and the playwright's art. The art of such navigation entails hermeneutical thinking which does not stop at the close of the text, but rushes into the seemingly sound foundations of the political ideals and arrangements in our own lives, washing away their edifying glamour and exposing the incongruities within. This sort of education is difficult. Just like philosophy and poetry, it is an art which, as the chorus of the *Knights* tells us, "many have courted [but] . . . few have enjoyed" (519–20).[47]

CHAPTER 4

Failures of High-Minded Politics: *Republic* VI and the *Birds*

On Reading and Education—A Prelude

It would appear that there is a difference between an education that trains our minds to grasp the products of someone else's thinking—be they ideas, concepts, formulas, principles, or methodologies—and the sort of learning that develops our own capacity for thought. The former produces technicians, as Foucault calls those who pass down the knowledge they profess to have.[1] The latter is difficult to pin down except by way of an example.

René Descartes, whose famous saying forever weds existence and a certain kind of thinking, gives us a clue to what learning how to think might look like. In the 1642 edition of the *Meditations*, Descartes's "Preface to the Reader" holds advice for those who seek to be persuaded not by judgments of authority, nor by appeasement of the views they already hold, but rather through careful reading and their own understanding of the text. To this audience alone Descartes addresses himself as an "author," and he asks that it "be able and willing to meditate seriously with" him.[2] What does it mean to undergo—through reading—the experience that might afford us an insight into Descartes's thought? Whatever that experience might be, it does not amount to simply breaking down the structure of Descartes's arguments or to setting—ahead of our understanding of the text—his "theory" of the dualism between the mind and the body. The latter brutally imposes a foreign meaning upon Descartes's language, which clarifies the way in which the two are distinct only to reiterate their intimate connection.[3] The author of the *Meditations* hearkens back, in the opening sentence of the "Preface," to the *Discourse on Method* "published in French in the year 1637."[4] Its fourth part holds a tightly wound kernel of Descartes's metaphysics. The first words of the *Discourse on Method of Conducting One's Reason Well and Seeking Truth in the Sciences* invite us to wonder about the ubiquity (or perhaps only seeming ubiquity) of "good sense."[5] From a disjunctive reading of the opening lines of the *Discourse*, and contrary to a straightforward take on Descartes's text, it follows that Descartes does not assume that we, the readers, possess the "power of judging well and of distinguishing the true from the false, which is properly what is called good sense or reason."[6] However, Descartes does not propose that he can teach us this capacity, as the self-assured claims of the popular curricula of "critical thinking" do today. Instead, the thinker claims, "it is not my intention here to teach the method that each should follow to conduct his reason well, but only to show in what fashion I have tried to conduct my own."[7] We might assume that in order to learn Descartes's method, we would need to imitate the author's procedure and path, but things are not that simple. Descartes goes on to say: "I offer this writing as a history, or if you prefer, as a fable, in which among some examples that can be imitated, there will perhaps be found also many others that it will not be right to follow."[8]

In the *Meditations*, then, the subject of Descartes's address is someone able to dispose herself toward the text in such a way as to engage in the meditative practice. Induced by Descartes's words, this practice would bear fruit if it ignited in the reader—at least momentarily—the insight that sustained Descartes's thought and that is preserved in his writings. In the *Discourse*, Descartes calls upon a discerning reader; that is, someone who does not aim at copying either Descartes's precepts and maxims or his experiences and ideas. Rather, he calls upon someone who realizes from the start that a careful reading of the *Discourse on Method* is already an undergoing. This undergoing is an experience in its own right. It leads the reader to espy in the form of Descartes's writing the very method and procedure of his thought. Sensitivity to the form in this case is part and parcel of one's understanding of the content. Descartes recommends that in order to be a sensible reader of the *Discourse*, one ought to engage in a discourse with the text.

Descartes presents his work to us as a history or as a fable, that is, as a text that abides by the poetic and dramatic form of the *as if*. The latter is important, because it would amount to nonsense if we took it to be advisable to do or think as Praxagora or Hamlet do. It would also be strange if we seriously believed that our reading about the lives and works of Cleopatra or Socrates could make us be like them. Thus, the idea that if we understand Descartes's experiments and repeat his experiences, then we will have knowledge of his thoughts, is equally erroneous. The reading of a discourse, just as the reading of a dialogue, does not aim at boxing in ideas or establishing the veracity of arguments based on an initial assessment of their logical consistency. This is not what learning *how* to think looks like. Descartes, who speaks in the first person, is more charitable than Plato (of the dialogues) in the advice he gives on the matter of learning how to read and how to think. It is worth repeating that the *Discourse* is "a fable, in which, among some examples that can be imitated, there will perhaps be found also many others that it will not be right to follow."[9] Note that Descartes does not tell us which examples we should take up and which ones we should set aside. At least one reason for this is the person of the reader and the inimitable character of the experiences, thoughts, reflections, and insights that she brings into the conversation with the text. Descartes confirms this conjecture when his own words, in the *Discourse*, retrace those of Plato in *Republic* VI. I cite the passage from the *Discourse* first: "For it is not enough to have a good mind [*l'esprit*], but the principal thing is to apply it well. The greatest souls [*âmes*] are capable of the greatest vices as well as the greatest virtues, and those who only walk very slowly can advance much further, if they always follow the right path, than those who run and go astray."[10]

And now in the *Republic*, addressing Adeimantus, Socrates asks: "Won't we say for souls [*psychas*] too . . . that, similarly, those with the best natures [*euphuestatas*] become exceptionally bad when they get bad instruction?" (491e). Socrates goes on, "Or do you suppose an ordinary nature is the source of great injustices and unmixed villainy? Don't you suppose, rather, that it's a lusty one corrupted by its rearing, while a weak nature [*asthenê de phusin*] will never be the cause of great things either good or bad?" (491e).[11] It is striking how close Descartes comes to Plato's Socrates on this matter of the relationship between education and personality—what the thinkers call one's "soul." Descartes thinks about learning in terms of travels or traversals of life's path. I would undo my own analysis if I were simply to agree with the second half of Descartes's statement, because I would be disregarding his suggestion to read the *Discourse* as if it were a fable. Fables are not prescriptive, they do not offer plans to be implemented in life, but instead guide the soul by offering signs, metaphors, and riddles to which no one-size-fits-all solution can be found. For some who, like Descartes himself (a Renaissance *Theorôs*), possess a quick as well as a reflective mind, and who are also fond of travel, it is advisable to both move along the so-called "right path" and to wander off this course. This two-pronged method of traversing philosophical texts offers a third vantage point. From this position, each reader or interlocutor who holds her own discourse with the text can understand whether, why, and how the opposing or disjunctive views, arguments, and propositions about ways of thinking (as well as ways of life) are evaluated as being either "good" or "bad," "correct" or "erroneous." Such an immersive reading is deeply theoretical because it is both a practice or an undergoing and a meditative, that is, a reflective exercise. This method follows along the lines of interpreters of Plato's dialogues such as Seth Benardete, Leo Strauss, Rachel Barney, Arlene Saxonhouse, Jill Frank, Cinzia Arruzza, John Sallis, Drew Hyland, Ronna Burger, Bernard Freydberg, Debra Nails, Jacob Howland, and Mauro Bonazzi.

Following these authors in their attentiveness to the dramatic and literary texture of Plato's texts, I advocate the view that Plato's characters are stylized and that to read Plato carefully means to attempt to understand Plato's choices of the dialogical cast. The analysis of the historical, literary, and dramatic constitution of the dialogical exchanges situates the discussions about education, politics, and metaphysics that we find in the *Republic.* To wit, the high-minded and the highfalutin prescriptions and ideals that Socrates sets up through the course of the exchanges about the best city (Kallipolis), the education of the guardians, and the status and role of the philosopher-kings are all tools by means of which Socrates aims to win his aristocratic interlocutors—Adeimantus and Glaucon—over to his side. These rhetorical and psychological tools that Plato has Socrates employ are partially reflections of his interlocutors' personality (they have to be in order to be even nominally effective), and partially they are distortions or inflated representations of the ideals, desires, and ideas of some of the actual Athenians of Plato's time. These are dramatic images—like those we want to contemplate in *Aida* or *Macbeth*. The elucidation of the role of dramatic characters in Plato, and the conceptualization of the role of drama in a philosophical work, allow us to see that taking any of the *Republic*'s political constructs or educational dictums prescriptively means barring ourselves from a coherent understanding of the text.[12] None of the educational advice issued to Glaucon is meant prescriptively and simply for the reader. Then why is it there at all?

Socrates's pedagogy unfolds before our eyes in the way that Pierre Bezukhov's education in the Masonic doctrines gradually unfolds in Tolstoy's *War and Peace*. We read about Pierre's studies and we see how they take root in him and how they affect his soul. However, we would miss the point of Tolstoy's narrative if we decided that, like Pierre, we must become Freemasons. Similarly in the *Republic*, Socrates and the interlocutors put on display their ideas about education in order that we may study the gradual becoming of the desired character that this educational program promises to mold upon completion. However, given that this education applies to the inhabitants of the city in speech (this education is not proposed for any real city), we should be cautious, lest we hastily adopt its proposed means and ends. In the following section, I indicate the outcomes of this conversational education.

Kallipolis for Whom?

Socrates speaks with Adeimantus about the training and education of those who will secure the stability of the best regime. Adeimantus had taken over the conversation from Glaucon at 487a, immediately after Glaucon mentioned Momus, a god of ridicule, a joker, and a critic of the Olympian gods. Now that Socrates has given an account of equality between the guardian women and men; of the communal belonging of all women and children to men; as well as the precarious final requirement that rulers must philosophize or that philosophers must rule, he is setting out to speak about "what concerns the rulers . . . as it were, from the beginning" (502e).

We recall that this conversation, at least for Socrates, offers a bird's-eye view of the proposed city. He is its most prolific founder as he supplies ideas about which kinds of practices, laws, and customs will constitute the makeup of the new regime. Having instilled in his interlocutors the belief that the philosopher is the best ruler, Socrates now equates the "most precise [*akribestatous*] guardian" (503b) with the philosopher. There is an opportunity for those guardians who stick to their training and who most accurately resemble the exemplary representatives of their class to rise up through the ranks. The proposed selection method by means of which one could be inducted into the rulers' creed involves training and trials of the body, mind, and soul. Socrates reminds us that the "rulers . . . must show themselves to be lovers of the city, tested [*basanidzomenous*] in pleasures and pains," and that, moreover, they must not "cast out this conviction in labors or fears" (503a). This statement about trials is repeated again shortly, where it qualifies the nature (*phusis*, 503b) that the "precise guardians" must possess. Their nature must be "tested [*basanisteon*] in the labors, fears, and pleasures we mentioned then. Moreover—what we passed over then but mention now—they must also be given gymnastic in many studies, to see whether [their nature] . . . will be able to bear the greatest studies" (503e). The sort of test that would determine whether one is fit to rule indicates fitness both in terms of one's public life ("lovers of the city," 503a) and in terms of one's private dispositions (pleasures, pains, fears, labors, 503a–b). The law-giving founders of the city (497b–c) have already agreed in private conversation that it is needful to administer these tests (503b, 504a) if the promising members of the community are to have any chance at ruling in the best way (i.e., philosophically) and, thereby, safeguarding the best regime.

This is interesting not the least because the exact same arrangement—where a young man who has a "philosophic nature" (495a), must be prodded on and tested by the dwellers of actual cities—was deemed ruinous not so long ago in the dialogue. In a passage that underscores the damaging effects of the trials that a youth undergoes while training, Socrates tells Adeimantus that if "thanks to his good nature and his kinship to such speeches, one young man were to apprehend something and be turned and drawn toward philosophy, what do we suppose those will do who believe they are losing his use and comradeship?" (494e). Socrates then asks: "Is there any deed they won't do or any word they won't say, concerning him, so that he won't be persuaded, and [won't they speak also about] the man who's doing the persuading, so that he won't be able to persuade; and won't they organize private plots and public trials?" (494e). The public trials (*dêmosia eis agônas*) and private plots (*idia epibouleuontas*), as Socrates presents the matter here, would corrupt the philosophically minded person. All else being equal, the difference between Socrates's prescription and his earlier prohibition of the same methods turns on three things. The first is the difference between the cities (one being actual, another being the best). The second difference is that between Socrates of the *Republic* and everyone else who is seeking to win over the talented young man. The third disjunction is indicated by the direction in which the youth's interests develop. Socrates presumably endorses a philosophical life of a talented youth, whereas his "kinsmen and fellow citizens" (*hoi te oikeioi kai hoi politai*, 494b) work to draw the young person away from philosophy. At least we must assume this is the case based on what the passage mentioned earlier (495a) most readily suggests. The young man would be drawn toward philosophy by the founders and lawgivers of the best regime.

By the time Plato is composing the *Republic* (in the first quarter of the fourth century B.C.E.), the fates of several talented young men who associated with Socrates and over whose souls—at least in the dialogues—we see him compete are sealed.[13] Some of them met a violent end, after having led lives of which the Socrates of the *Republic* is unlikely to have approved. Socrates himself was executed after having been found guilty of impiety and corruption of the young. Perhaps these tragic events would not have transpired if the Athenians, by magic or persuasion, had turned into the denizens of Socrates's best regime. Put this way, the suggestion is laughable because of its patent implausibility, to which history attests. Why, then, did Plato pen the passages about the Kallipolis, the education of the guardians, and the philosophers who are also kings? Having an ear for comedy, he must have known just how "funny" they would sound. We would have to be immensely (if not blindly and mistakenly) trusting to take on faith the speeches of Socrates, who adapts his models, concepts, and ideas to the particular interlocutor with whom he speaks. If we did, we would lose our own discursive perspective—the vantage point from which to judge the soundness of the prescriptions issued by Socrates regarding the "regime about which we tell tales in speech [*muthologoumen logô*] [so as to see] . . . its completion in deed [*ergo telos lêpsetai*]" (501e).

I bring to my dialogical engagement with Plato's dialogue another interlocutor—the one whose humorous escapades and comedic excurses magnify Plato's comedy, and thereby also suggest ways to understand his ridicule of certain kinds of political and educational ideas. In the *Republic* there are two ideas which are not meant to be brought to life, but which rather offer a comedic critique of particular and persistent human passions, beliefs, and desires. These two ideas are (1) the best regime and (2) its philosophical founders, who are well poised to be the rulers in it. The next section discusses the origin of the political ideals in the *Republic* and the *Birds*. In both texts, these origins belie the desire to live a halcyon and completely trouble-free, but not dishonorable life. This predilection for a life of pleasure and distinction, as well as the consequent outcomes this penchant has for politics, are easier to detect in the *Birds*. However, I will argue that the rulers of the best regime in the city in speech, which the dialogical characters build in the *Republic*, must be just as interested in pleasures and honors as the makers of the new regime in the *Birds*.

The Founders of the New Cities—Sex, Law, and Honor in the *Republic* and the *Birds*

The opening of the *Republic* and the opening of the *Birds* appear to indicate two opposite directions. Sallis provides several pieces of evidence for his claim that the "*Republic* begins with *Socrates' descent into Hades*."[14] The comedy, on the other hand, opens with the search for one Tereus, a king whose spattered personal history and rapacious desire led to his transformation into a "Hoopoe-Bird" (16).[15] To find this creature, two searchers, Peisthetairos and Euelpides, have armed themselves with birds—a jackdaw and a crow. Both birds end up taking the two elderly men outside of Athens. At a place that neither of them finds to be familiar (9), the birds give their sign and that is–up! (49–51). Heraclitus's saying holds true both for the *Republic*, where descent into Hades lays the ground for several ascents, and for the *Birds*, where, while aiming for the high-life of the birds, the characters are—from the start—on the road to the underworld. Peter Meineck remarks on the desolation of the no-man's land with which the play opens.[16] We see it as a visual image of the two old men's wish "to go to the birds," which in fifth-century Greek means "to go to hell."[17] The upward thrust which marks the opening of the *Birds* and will eventuate in the founding of the sky-high bird city—is also the road down. The glorious city in the heavens, in which Peisthetairos eventually comes to hold absolute rule, is Aristophanes's symbol for a plutocratic regime where a select few, or perhaps even a self-appointed one, enjoy tremendous splendor while the others suffer under the yoke of tyranny. Likewise, Kallipolis and the education and training prescribed by its founders for those who are meant to enjoy life in the best city, might hold a similar commentary on our penchant for power and our love of leisure, the latter being, of course, and no less precariously, a prerequisite for a philosophical life.

Socrates reverses the course of philosophical education from its form in the actual cities—or more specifically, we must assume, from an actual city of Athens—to the shape that he thinks it should take if the best regime, in which philosophers rule, is to come to pass. Socrates, speaking to Adeimantus, indicates that instead of learning philosophical matters in youth and in passing, one ought to wait until one's ripe age, and only then engage in the serious study of philosophy. At that point, "when the strength begins to fail and they are beyond political and military duties . . . they ought to be let loose to graze and do nothing else, except as a spare-time occupation" (498b–c). This leisure is for the sake of the philosophical life; this is the conclusion suggested by the context of the passage. However, Socrates ends his excursus on the proposed changes in the education and training of citizens under the best regime not by detailing the philosophical pursuits of the old, but by saying that their free-roaming, leisurely lifestyle will make the aged blessed at the end of this life and in the next (*tous mellontas eudaimonôs biôsesthai kai teleutêsantas*, 498c). This is a promise of an idyllic habitation untroubled by the various duties which an actual city-life calls for. Such a place that is free from cares and away from the busy Athenian life is exactly what the aged companions are searching for in the opening scene of the *Birds* (13–47).

Whereas, in the dialogue Socrates would have the celebrated elderly citizens be excused from the business of the city, in the comedy the two old men take it upon themselves to be relieved from their onerous affairs in Athens. Strauss's remarks on the opening lines of the *Birds* are telling and are worth quoting at length. He observes that the *Birds* is "the only Aristophanean play whose entire action takes place far from Athens. . . . It opens with a dialogue between two Athenian citizens who present themselves as such. These two men,"[18] who Strauss says are "Euelpides (Hopeful or the son of Hopeful) and Peisthetairos (a hybrid of 'persuader of his comrade' and 'trustworthy comrade')—have literally turned their backs on the city. They are prompted by the desire to escape from the restlessness or busybodyness of that grand city, and especially from the perpetual litigation, to a place or a city that is tranquil."[19] Moreover, Strauss says, "they wish to become members of a tranquil city already in existence, more tranquil even than the most tranquil city known to them, but perhaps at the same time as grand as Athens: a tranquil Athens. Since they know of no such place, they wish to find out from Tereus where they might find it."[20] Such a city has no lawsuits, nor does it embroil a wizened old man in its many and messy relations, dealings, and responsibilities. However, this city is celebrated for its glory all the same. It is a place where one no longer has to work hard to be deemed worthy of honors and all the enjoyments that are offered up to a preeminent citizen of this honorable polis. One might object that this could not possibly be what Socrates has in mind when he speaks of the leisurely life of the old in the best city, because in the best city one has to earn such a life. True though this is, recall that in the conversation that Socrates and Adeimantus have about law in book IV, the legislative, corrective, and litigious practices are compared to a sickness that corrupts the regime (425c–427a, 464d–e). The best city, once its laws have been established, is supposed to be quite tranquil as far as the business of law is concerned.

The best city is also supposed to edify its best citizens, granting to them a status and honors that surpass even those accorded to the "Olympic victors" (465d–466a, 469a–b). The conversations outline the prizes and pleasures (including erotic pleasures) that outstanding citizens of the Kallipolis deserve. Indeed, Glaucon is adamant about legalizing certain sexual pleasures and relations. He wants to "add to the new law that as long as they [best warriors] are on that campaign, no one whom he wants to kiss [*boulêtai philein*] be permitted to refuse, so that if a man happens to love [*tis tou tuchê erôn*] someone, either male or female, he would be more eager to win the rewards of valor" (468b–c). This is no innocent kissing that Glaucon has in mind. Moreover, the best warriors, of whom Glaucon fancies he might be one, will be allowed to "use their catch [*tê agra*] as they wish" (468a), much like the storied warriors who fought at Troy. The language here is that of catching prey, as one would on a hunting expedition. Aside from hearkening the Kallipolis back to the initially censored parts of the Homeric epos, this imagery evokes wild, untamed desires. Glaucon eagerly accepts the stipulation that the "man who proved best and earned a good reputation must first be crowned [*stephanôthênai*] by each of those who made the campaign with him, youths and boys [*meirakiôn te kai paidôn*] in turn" (468b). Our contemporary sensibility bids us to be worried about the possible relations the warriors may have with these accompanying children. The most beautiful city is only the best in name. The name hides the inner inconsistency of a regime in which the guardians are prescribed to practice moderation, in order to reap the reward that would allow them to satisfy their sexual desires immoderately and even violently if they wish. One cannot be both moderate and act on immoderate desires or act on one's sexual desires immoderately. The ground that holds up the best city is shaky. It threatens to erupt with violent, unruly, and tyrannically immoderate eros.

In Aristophanes's play, the wish that the two old men envision coming to fruition outside of the Athenian walls and law is no less playfully expressed, and is no less disturbing. The defectors from the polis agree that they are searching for "the same kind of thing," and that is

> a place where the father of some pretty young boy [*paidos hôraiou*] would come up to me and complain [*mempsetai hôsper adikêtheis*] saying, "Hey, twinkle-toes, That's no way to treat my son, he told me that you bumped into him outside the gym and you never tried to give him a little kiss [*ouk ekusas*] or a cuddle, and what's more, you didn't even bounce his balls! And you call yourself a friend of the family!" (137–43)[21]

Both searchers wish that they could live out their old age in a community where it is unjust *not* to fondle shapely children (*paidos hôraiou*, 138). Glaucon would agree that this sexual promiscuity should be welcomed.

In its fundamental attitude toward law, honor, and pleasure, as well as the dealings among the citizen-classes, the city that Euelpides and Peisthetairos are seeking is the city that Socrates and his interlocutors end up founding in speech. The mythical stock of the comedy offers a sinister commentary on one's desire to dwell in such a city.

We learn that Tereus, whom the elders seek at the beginning of the play, is the king of Thrace.[22] He marries an Athenian, a daughter of King Pandion. Her name is Procne. Her sister, who Tereus desires, is named Philomela. Tereus gets his way with Philomela and then cuts out her tongue to forestall accusations. A crafty woman, Philomela weaves tapestries that tell the story of her suffering. These picture tales make their way into the hands of Procne, who conspires with her sister to kill Tereus's child, Itylus—her own son. The body of Itylus is cooked into a sumptuous meal and served to the boy's father, who only realizes what transpired when the women display the child's head to the king. The gods see to it that all four—Tereus, Philomela, Procne, and Itylus—suffer a metamorphosis by changing into birds that are, respectively, a hoopoe, a nightingale, a swallow, and a pheasant.

Lest we be inclined to dismiss the bloody terror of Tereus's crime and misfortune as some peculiar but insignificant detail, Aristophanes brings this account to full circle at the close of the *Birds*. Peisthetairos, the self-appointed ruler of the bird-city that he founds, feasts on the choicest and juiciest of the birds—the ones who are found guilty of not being friendly enough to the city's regime (1579–85). Strauss takes the description of the "rich, fat, or juicy" birds to mean that "some aristocratic . . . birds have been condemned to death by the democrats. . . . Yet the birds' regime is a democracy only in name; in fact it is the rule of the first man."[23] Whereas, Tereus dines on the body of his son in ignorance of the horrendous act, Peisthetairos devours the citizens of Nephelokokkygia (Cloudcuckooland) quite knowingly and with no remorse. The rule by which Peisthetairos holds power in the high-walled city (1125–65) is tyranny.[24]

Absolute Rule of the Tyrannical Elite in Cloudcuckooland and in Kallipolis

Although in the *Republic* tyranny enters the discussion explicitly only in book VIII, and unlike in the *Birds*, democracy in the *Republic* rather is closest to the tyrannical but not to the best regime, we must observe that the best regime does not shun violence or manipulation. The rulers of the Kallipolis do not tolerate insubordination and seek to breed it out (429c–430a) to such an extent that in its final shape, according to Socrates, the interlocutors have an "obedient city" (*polin echôn peithomenên*, 502b). The plan of the best regime in its arrangement, legal structure, and its daily life is only conspicuous to those who rule (458b–459c, 459e–460a). Moreover, the founders of the city do not shy away from telling lies—true lies [*alethôs pseudos*, 382a]—to the city dwellers (382e–d, 459c–d). In such a city, Howland tells us, the tyrannically minded Critias, one of Glaucon's older lovers, "would feel entirely at home."[25]

The historical Critias, possessed of a "deceptive and manipulative . . . mind,"[26] was a man whose aristocratic lineage ran six generations deep, and who played a great part in the fate of Glaucon. Far from cauterizing the tyrannical affinities of the aristocratic men whom he enlists in the construction of the best regime (427c), Socrates weaves the ideas, desires, and things that such men as Critias (who was one of the most violent members of the pro-Spartan Thirty Tyrants) happen to value into the fabric of the new city. In the *Republic*, Critias's glory- and pleasure-seeking impulses reach their fever pitch in the sex commune of the guardian warriors in the Kallipolis (459d–e), which Howland says is "a child born of the intellectual union of Thrasymachus and Glaucon" and, I add, this offspring is delivered to us by Socrates.[27] "Callipolis's citizens, if that is the right word, are crafted by rulers who possess an ostensibly precise and scientific knowledge of what is."[28] Howland concludes that "these philosopher-kings tightly control all forms of creative eroticism: sex is mathematically regulated, and poets are employed to fabricate religious myths and medicinal lies so as to conceal this fact."[29] Following Rosen, Howland finds difficulty in referring to the dwellers of the best city as "citizens."[30] His hesitation is warranted. After all, how could the dogs, the animals that Socrates uses over and again to describe the dispositions and life of the guardians, or "noble cocks" (459a), for that matter, be citizens of any city?

The distance is slim between a guardian-dog and the tyrannical ruler who comes onto the scene toward the end of the dialogue. Socrates compares the tyrant to a wolf (565d–e). By contrast, the distance between the founders of the best regime and its future denizens is insurmountable. Socrates and his interlocutors are human, and thus inhabit a plane that is altogether different from the one where animals, even domesticated animals like dogs, dwell. However, this difference does not preclude the untoward treatment that the suprahuman or supreme beings might impose upon the subordinate or "obedient" (502b) ones. Similarly, in the *Birds*, Peisthetairos, "the only man, among the birds, . . . is so firmly in the saddle that he does not have to forgo the eating of well-cooked and well-seasoned, if well-sentenced and well-executed birds."[31]

Historically speaking, all of these cookings and executions had already taken place by the time that Plato composed the *Republic*. The pro-Spartan oligarchs, who ruled tyrannically, purged Athens depriving choicest and most powerful of the Athenian citizens and *metics* of their status, wealth, and often, also, of their lives. During the conversations that make up Plato's *Politeia* (within the dramatic setting of the dialogue, that is) none of these atrocities had yet taken place. As Nails indicates, dramatically the *Republic* is probably set during the Peace of Nicias (421 B.C.E.).[32] We, however, are in a position to read the dialogue in the context of the postwar history of ancient Athens. As readers, we can contemplate—as if on a dramatic stage—the ideal (by which I mean the saturated and amplified) drives, impulses, and passions that (in our imaginations) might create such fantastical sights as the purest city or the best regime.

Besides being a regime in which kings who also philosophize are at the top, it is also a regime in which some members of the polis are simply not included in it apart from providing for the city's economic wellbeing. The artisans, who are supposedly the financial backbone of the city, are entirely prohibited from participating in its civic life. They provide the goods for the upper classes, but they do not engage in any of the religious, political, or community-building activities in which the auxiliaries, the guardians, and the kings engage. What is behind this interest that favors elitism in rule? Socrates ties Glaucon and Adeimantus to their aristocratic lineage by painstakingly articulating and adapting to the brothers' characters and beliefs that selfsame promise which Peisthetairos issues in the agon of the *Birds*—"that they can rule again by adopting his scheme."[33]

In the comedy, this scheme serves to endow its proponent with absolute rule. Peisthetairos marries Zeus's daughter Basileia, becoming effectively the ruler of the all (*ta panta kratesas*, 1753). In the *Republic*, marriage to the choicest member of the best regime is meant not for Socrates (who furnishes the conceptual framework for the construction of the Kallipolis) but for the best city's most distinguished guardians (459d–460a). Glaucon's inability to resist the various pleasures that are available to the choicest citizens of the Kallipolis shows that at least this dialogical character is won over by the idea that the most desirable marriage and whatever power that may come with it would be reserved for someone like himself.[34] In Aristophanes's play, the advantages that the coveted marriage might bring are incredible for a mortal because "through possessing Basileia, Peisthetairos will be the possessor of everything."[35] Aristophanes gives us an image of stupendous hubris. Although the men who give an account of the Kallipolis do not claim to oust Zeus, there are indications of the selfsame hubris at work in the dialogical ascent to the Good in the *Republic* (507a–509a). The next section lays bare the metaphysical presuppositions of tyrannical rule. These metaphysical doctrines culminate in the ascent to the Good, and I now offer an analysis of the political implications of this ascent.

The (Pseudo-) Metaphysical Foundations of Political Elitism

The study that culminates in the contemplation of the Idea of the Good (517b–c) proposes that the metaphysics (of the Good) underlies and guides ethical and political life. It takes Socrates the better part of book VII to articulate the steps of this endeavor. Once Socrates's interlocutors understand the procedure by which one can attain the proper training that would allow one to complete the ascent, they can then legislate the same curriculum as the education of the ruling class in the best city. These interlocutors include Glaucon, who reenters the conversation when Socrates moves to the discussion of the ascent. Meant exclusively for the guardians who are fit to be kings, the "*idea* of the good" (508e) "provides the truth to the things known and gives the power to the one who knows" (508e). Book VII spells out the careful study of such serious subjects as geometry, mathematics, astronomy, and dialectics, for example, as prerequisites for the highest knowledge that secures one's understanding of the phenomenal and epistemic structures of the world. However, all of these subjects bottleneck at the height which, by design, excludes anyone but the future rulers. Therefore, the select initiates may use their study and their averred knowledge in ways that could not be contested. The metaphysical insight (whatever it may be) that the ruling elite of the Kallipolis gains through its elevated education is the ground and the tool that is supposed to legitimize their political actions and their status as rulers. Religion, we observe, is second, at best, in reinforcing the power of the ruling elite. Socrates proposes nothing short of a supreme order in which the initiates rise up to a status that surpasses even the known gods. This is so because they are oriented and led in their "greatest study" (*tou megistou . . . mathêmatos*, 504d) by that which lies beyond Being (*epikeina tês ousias*, 509b), and therefore, beyond the divinities themselves. Seen from this perspective, the exalted education and knowledge that (according to Socrates) secure the correctness and power of the rulers in the best regime are "*hubris* just waiting to be punished."[36] Meineck concludes this about the denouement of the *Birds*.

The comedy's portrayal of the new regime, with Euelpides gone[37] and Peisthetairos having set himself up as the absolute ruler, intensifies the laughable and problematic character of the Kallipolis. Once it is founded, consecrated, and enclosed within a massive wall, Cloudcuckooland becomes a power-broker between human beings and the gods. At least that is the city's initial and overt position. However, this intermediary status changes quickly, and to the detriment of the divine beings.

Peisthetairos fails to keep his promises to the inhabitants of his city, that is, to the birds. Strauss sums it up saying that Peisthetairos wins the birds over to his cause when he instills in them a belief that "by occupying and fortifying the place between the heaven (the place of the gods) and the earth (the place of men), the birds will become the rulers of both gods and men, the universal rulers."[38] The only representative of this proposed new ruler class at the end is Peisthetairos himself. He does not appear to appease the gods, either. Instead, the play ends with Peisthetairos eclipsing Zeus, or at least approximating Zeus's power. Although the constitution makers who set up the Kallipolis in the *Republic* do not propose to oust Zeus and others, we see, using the example of the play, what might come to pass if the city in speech is brought to be in action.

If it were to come to pass, the philosopher-kings of the best regime would find themselves in a position not only to tell lies about divine sanctions (such as those approving of certain marriages, but prohibiting others), but also to take stock of the malleable character of seemingly unquestionable and unshakable divine laws. We know that instead of being lovers of the gods, the rulers in the Kallipolis are meant to be diviners of the Idea of the Good. But the Good, which is beyond Being, cannot be known. At least, it cannot be known in any discursive manner that would enable one to understand its content and its meaning, and then explain it to someone else. So it is hard to tell how the rulers in the best regime would be able to refrain from seeing to it that the Good (*agathos*) which regulates their rule is anything but a sophisticated version of the good (*agathos*) that Thrasymachus outlined to start (342e–344c).[39] The philosopher-kings are poised to end up ruling the Kallipolis as astute and well-trained social engineers (to use an anachronism). Their rule aimed at the preservation and reinforcement of the *politeia* and the polis would first and foremost serve themselves. How is this *not* an elaborate and crafty reiteration of Thrasymachus's slogan?[40] Socrates's version is all the more formidable because it considers some such self-undermining elements for which Thrasymachus fails to account. To wit, Socrates takes into his account the fact that the advantage of the ruler is intimately connected to the fates of the ruled. However, what evidence is there for thinking that Socrates's Kallipolis would be any better for the ruled than Thrasymachus's tyranny of "perfect injustice" (344a)? Whereas the latter considers the ruled to be sheep that are kept safe and fattened until the day of their slaughter, the Kallipolis indefinitely prolongs the subjugation of the artisans and their labor to the needs of the dwellers of the upper class. The city's dependence on the artisans for its survival and for the support of its militaristic exploits is undeniable, but the artisans' participation in the political and social life of the Kallipolis is nominal. The artisans are for the city, but the Kallipolis is not for them. The elitist rulers are very well educated, and they are exceptionally fit both physically and mentally. Their rule is perfectly just because it is underwritten by their true understanding of the idea of the Good. All of this sounds great, if it were not for the fact that this rule relies completely on the rulers' orientation toward that which is—by definition—unreachable because of its supra-ontological status. No creator of totalitarianism could hide the ends of absolute power quite this well.

Glaucon and Adeimantus are on board with Socrates's proposal, but this does not mean that we should be too. Like Cloudcuckooland, the Kallipolis originates in a simple city that beckons us with its elegant and just arrangement that is quite contrary to the litigious quagmire of actual city life. However, driven by the interests, beliefs, and desires of those citizens who are closest to rule (be they the aristocratically-minded oligarchs of ancient Athens, the elitists of the *Republic*, or the absolutists of Cloudcuckooland), the simple—and for all intents and purposes—impossible polis gives way to a revamped tyranny. We go in the *Republic* (and the movement of the *Birds* comically portrays and amplifies political unworthiness of the same path) from a demand for perfect justice unburdened by the many problems and blemishes of human, that is, finite and fallible life, to a utopic (or maybe a dystopic) place.

Infantile Longings and Political Terror

I now establish a direct relationship between the troubled life under tyranny and the desire for a completely trouble-free life. In summary, my conclusion turns on the fact that it is impossible to lead a life unburdened by the demands of politics. Yet if we wish for such a life, that is, a life that is fantastically and perhaps naively virginal in terms of its political engagements, then we expose ourselves to the worst kind of political manipulation. We suffer at the hands of those who want to wield great power. Founding and governing a city involves establishing laws, as well as nexuses of legal and political power that will continuously engage in the reassessment of the initial constitution. This is far from a simple and carefree life. Socrates's idyll—a simple city—is Euelpides's rustic community, where its dwellers could be "free as the birds" (34). Both the comedy and the dialogue show that such a city cannot be found, nor can it be founded. Peisthetairos serves as the legislator, thereby turning the new city into what begins to look a lot like another Athens, but with one man (that is, himself) at the top.[41] Euelpides flees the place. Athenians interested in circumventing the laws of Athens flock to Cloudcuckooland (e.g., 1280–85).[42] Euelpides and Peisthetairos in the comedy, and Socrates in the *Republic* replace the longing for a simpler and more carefree life—a longing that many human beings have—by an impossibly uncomplicated life. The sinister underbelly of the desire for such a pure community is that if we seek to express it by bringing this community to life, then we have not even begun to confront our deep-seated but unsavory longings and beliefs. Besides its being a glaring example of our unwillingness to learn about ourselves, this dream, which turned out to be dystopic, has been nightmarishly transferred onto the lives of real people (e. g., in Soviet Russia). To avail ourselves of this type of infantilism in politics and ethics would always mean to empower those who make it their business to understand the workings of the human psyche and use this knowledge toward their selfish ends. If we do not seek to know ourselves, then we put our lives at the mercy of those who might rely on their knowledge of human nature for the sake of manipulating rather than enlightening the public.

The step by which Socrates reintroduces multiple extravagances and vices into the simple city (372e–374e) is also a step that leads back to the actual city; namely, to our own sort of community. The inflamed, rather than the simple, city is the true city. It is true actually because it is true to life. A new regime, both in the dialogue and in the comedy, requires that the extant regime, the actual one, must undergo a purging. However, the purged or purified regime fails to deliver on a promise of idyllic life that is utterly free from vice, violence, and corruption. The idyllic city is just as impossible as the perfectly just person or regime. This idyll becomes a joke both in the *Birds* and in the *Republic*. It is meant to let us take stock of our overly romantic and idealized views of life. The perfectly just individual and regime hide tyranny, or rather, they are examples of the kind of unquestionable perfection that tyranny and tyrants hide behind when seeking to avoid accountability and culpability. Cloudcuckooland in the *Birds* treads close to history and makes explicit the ideas that the Kallipolis overshadows with its brilliance and might.[43] Peisthetairos, who rules like a tyrant, does not shun justice until it stands in the way of his own needs (1584–85). He cleverly dismisses the unjust father-beater, who yearns to be like the high-flying birds, that is, to have wings and soar above the ancestral prohibition against patricide (1344–70). Peisthetairos also sends the shyster, the double-dealing court informant (*sykophantês*), away (1410–65). However, in upholding the idea of justice for those interested in being the citizens of Cloudcuckooland, Peisthetairos is not himself just. Strauss asks whether Peisthetairos "reserves for himself alone the power to act unjustly with impunity."[44] Socrates, the persuasive companion to the Athenian youth—the man who advocates the need to have an "obedient city" (*polin echôn peithomenên*, 502b)—does not prescribe that the subsequent generations of philosopher-kings be held accountable to a high tribunal.

CHAPTER 5

No Laughing Matter: Tyranny in *Republic* VIII and IX

I have argued thus far that if we take the dialogical accounts about politics and education exactly as they appear in the city in speech and apply them to life, then we miss the point of the *Republic* entirely. If we were to attempt such a transposition, we would certainly make our life more tragic. I have also argued that to read Plato means to enter into a dialogue with his text. Plato's dialogues are occasions for philosophizing, which goes hand in hand with self-examination. If we fail to examine ourselves—our opinions and predilections—then we are likely to adopt those views and ideas which best align with our own. However, not every well-established opinion is in fact the best one. We can see Plato's silence on the matter of his own beliefs (that is, his authorial choice of the dialogical style) as an encouragement to always examine ours. Charles Griswold says that "*Platonic anonymity . . . attests to the core meaning of philosophy as questioning directed to self-knowledge.*"[1]

In Aristophanes's comedy, the ignorance of characters often causes laughter. This ignorance belongs, at least to some extent, to us as well. Comedic levity facilitates our capacity to laugh at ourselves—at our follies and shortcomings. Every such moment of self-directed laughter is an occasion to take note of our own weaknesses, our ignorance, our vices and limitations. In this way, comedy invites us to engage in self-examination. But what is the relationship between self-knowledge and tyranny, which is hardly a laughing matter? In this chapter I take my cue from Plato's Socrates, who leaves the question of his own nature (whether it is gentle or violent) undecided. Socrates claims that since he does not know about himself and his own nature, he must abide by the dictum of Apollo which says "*Gnôthi Seauton.*" This ambivalence on Socrates's part recommends to all readers of Plato that we always seek to examine ourselves. The arguments that I lay out in this chapter claim that self-knowledge and tyranny pursue divergent paths. Nonetheless, both tyrannical tendencies and the capacity for self-examination belong to human nature. This means that in barring the pursuit of self-knowledge, we are bound to either follow tyrannical ideologies or lead tyrannical ways of life ourselves.

If the philosopher-kings of the best regime rule tyrannically, then tyranny is neither the furthest from the best regime, nor is it four times removed from aristocracy. This result runs contrary to the gradation of the regimes which the interlocutors discuss in the concluding books of the *Republic*. In this chapter, I will show how it is the case that these forms of government bleed into one another.[2] An eidetic analysis helps to separate them out, but this misleads us if we seek to apply such a strict separation to life. In the actual life of Plato's time (and thereafter) we do not meet with such an organization of state, wherein the various forms of government are neatly compartmentalized and sufficiently distinct from one another. The reason for a strict organization of regimes in *Republic* VIII–IX has to do with the manner in which the forms of regimes are staked to the shapes of the soul. Not only is it plausible that in the best regime there could be tyrannically minded people, but more importantly, it seems wildly hubristic to assume that any one of us is fully and forever devoid of tyrannical desires, inclinations, and thoughts. If Plato's Socrates could not quite tell about himself whether he had a terrible or a gentle nature, then this makes both his interlocutors and us (the readers of the dialogues) wonder whether we are immune to wild, tyrannical passions and whether we can exercise—in most decisive situations—perfect self-possession and control. I study this image of "Typhonic Socrates" in the next section in order to prepare the ground for my analysis of our own Typhonic inclinations—be they our excessive passions, our untamed desires, our prejudices, or our moral faults. I carry out this study because these darker aspects of ourselves are just as formative of who we are as our noble, moderate, and reasonable inclinations. Moreover, and perhaps unexpectedly, our colloquially "better" selves are not immune from guiding our decisions toward overly idealistic and, therefore, shortsighted ends. In short, to study ourselves as Socrates does is to engage in the search for self-knowledge, and as Griswold explains, such a search is indispensable to "leading one's life in the best possible way."[3]

Typhonic Socrates

In the *Phaedrus*, an image of Socrates—an image of his character's function in Plato's dialogues—is cast in the shape of a "wild beast more twisted and in spirit more furious than Typhon" (*thêrion on . . . Tuphônos poluplokôteron kai mallon epitethummenon*, 230a). This image is framed by Socrates's questioning of himself. The reason why the monster appears is that Socrates "cannot yet, according to the Delphic inscription, know" (*ou dunamai pô kata to Delfikon gramma gnônai emauton*, 229e) himself and cannot tell whether he is monstrous or whether he is a "tame and simple animal, partaking in the divine and modest part [in life] by nature" (*hêmerôteron te kai haplousteron zoôn, theias tinos kai atuphou moiras phusei metechon*, 230a). Socrates's choice of the figure of Typhon is telling. In Greek mythology, the latter was a progenitor (along with Echidna) of several remarkably monstrous creatures. Hesiod reports that Typhon fathered Cerberus, Lernean Hydra, and Chimera.[4] The Nemean lion and the Sphinx were the offspring of Orthus and Echidna, according to Hesiod; but Apollodorus writes that Typhon and Echidna begat the Sphinx.[5] Socrates presents himself as being uncertain, at least while speaking with Phaedrus, about his own nature. He could be tame and simple, but he could also be hubristic and even more rapacious than Typhon. Socrates is ambiguous about the nature and character of his eros and the fruits of its labor. Moreover, the matter of his nature and his (and our) knowledge thereof is so far from being settled that Socrates finds it necessary to alert Phaedrus to its dangerous possibilities. There is a hubristic, tyrannical monstrosity that looks a lot like a Typhonic monstrosity. The latter points to the monstrous complexity of Socrates's character.

In view of these images of the monstrous, one is well advised not to discount them as being in every way and necessarily bad—that is, destructive, vicious, and harmfully unnatural—when one comes upon them in Plato's dialogues or in life. The monstrosity of tyranny does not necessarily stem from a Socrates-like complexity. Nonetheless, if the tyrannical characters are labeled "bad" and left unstudied, then we ourselves become the vehicles of narrow-minded confusion. Instead, to try to see both the complex and the twisted possibilities of our own souls is what both the Socratic Typhon and the tyrant of the *Republic* call on us to do. The attitude that one assumes when embarking on these soul searches is important. In questioning oneself—in pressing against the limits that trace one's human nature—one is in a position to discover what those limits are. Seeing where and how one would become monstrous if one were to cross a certain boundary is not the same as simply abiding by the established moral standards of the day. Nor is it an act of setting aside, avoiding, or repressing the uncomfortable limits. There is a promise of guidance and a call to probe one's depths, as well as one's shallowness, in the study of the many-figured movements of Plato's dialogues.[6] There is a chance to reckon with what is most one's own. To do that one must also face what seems to be most foreign to oneself. One has to look at the design that could be one's own particular monster.

Gravely Serious—Tyrannical Ideology

I now unite my analysis of the importance of self-knowledge with the shortsightedness (not to say utter blindness) of tyranny. I also explain why comedy—if it is well received—is both an occasion for a reflection upon oneself and a powerful agent in combating political tyranny. The concluding books of the *Republic* are anything but lighthearted. At their most serious, the exchanges turn to the consideration of tyranny. The passion which is called "tyrannical eros" (*eros tyrannos*, 573d) is a phrase that Plato himself coined in the fourth century B.C.E.

Whether he means to or not, Plato unites Pericles's and Cleon's addresses to the Athenian citizens. Thucydides reports that Pericles in 431 B.C.E. called on the Athenians to become the polis's lovers (*alla mallon tên tês poleôs dunamin kath' hêmeran ergo theômenous kai erastas gignomenous autês*).[7] In 427 B.C.E., two years after Pericles's death, Cleon chided the Athenians for their blindness to the fact that their reign in the region is thoroughly tyrannical (*ou skopountes hoti tyrannida echete tên archên*).[8] If Athens wields a tyrannical power, then in order to be her lover, one has to love tyranny. Putting these two remarks together, Plato writes Socrates's speech, in which love and tyranny join forces to yield a terrible kind of eros, that is, a love of tyranny and a tyrannical love. Plato's Socrates makes this passion responsible for a lawless and anarchical life (*anarchia kai anomia zôn*, 575a).[9]

Tyrannos, a word that traveled to ancient Greece from the southwestern Balkan peninsula in the mid-seventh century B.C.E., is an equivalent to *basileus*.[10] Initially, *tyrannos* differed from *basileus*, which describes hereditary kingship, only in this—the tyrant seizes power, rather than inheriting it. The word *tyrannos* was first used in Greece by Archilochus, whose poetic character, the carpenter Charon, rejects the wealth and tyranny wielded by the Lydian king Gyges. *Tyrannos* originally had a positive meaning, at best, but more probably an ambivalent one.[11] A century later, by the time that Solon was composing, the word was aligned with the violence directed against the people by a tyrant, as well as with the violence a tyrant eventually suffers when he is overthrown. A connection between lowly birth and the tyrant's illegitimate ascent to power became established, and "tyranny" acquired an unambiguously negative connotation. By the time Sophocles presented his tragedy *Oedipus* (hypothesized to have been first performed between 428–425 B.C.E.), "tyranny" was identified with hubris and with terror.[12]

Books VIII and IX of the *Republic* trace the changes in the communal life shared by the rulers and the people in order to show how "tyranny grows naturally out of the root of leadership" (*phuêtai tyrannos, ek prostatikês rhitzês*,

565d). In Plato's work, it is no longer in question that tyranny has transformed from a benign to an abhorrent kind of rule. Given the historical events through which Plato lived, it is hard to believe that he would have considered tyranny a good subject for a joke. However, the analyses of Plato's comedy I have offered make it equally difficult to equate the intention of the author with the advice issued by his literary creation, Socrates of the dialogues, who advocates as early as book II in the *Republic* that the guardians of the best city "shouldn't be lovers of laughter" (*oude philogelôtas ge dei einai*, 388e). Why would the budding tyranny, whether of a private or a public kind, make itself more conspicuous if we study it through the lens of laughter?

The sorts of public sentiments that a tyrannical government (whether of socially democratic or of conservatively elitist cast) relies on and seeks to foment are passionate idealism and nationalism. The political agendas that express these passions in concrete terms may strive for diametrically opposed visions of society (e.g., the brotherhood of the international proletariat, on the one hand, or xenophobic protectionism, on the other). Their slogans may differ wildly, but the attitude excited in the supporters of these politically framed ideas is the same. It is an attitude of grave, unwavering seriousness. The social background, economic standing, and level of education of the supporters hardly matter. Tyrannical ideologues draw on and manipulate something that runs deeper still within us. Our passions. And even if our passions can be educated, which is still—even for those who consider themselves to be highly educated—a very big "if," they cannot be rooted out. If they could, we would be dehumanized entirely.

Guided by some such intuition and a worry that a passion of great hatred was rising in the world, Albert Einstein turned to Sigmund Freud for an answer to the question that deplorably is no less pressing now, and that is: "Why War?"[13] In our choice of peace at times of sweltering discord, Einstein trusted the public at large as much as or even more than he trusted the intellectual elite. His reasoning for this was simple—the men of letters lead a life that is unsoiled by "direct contact with life in the raw."[14] Lacking such firsthand knowledge, they are all the more susceptible to flights of fancy that end up glorifying and proposing as desirable the images of life that history has proven to be violent, destructive, and vile if brought to life. Despite their highbrow views, the intellectual elite are just as likely to support terror as the half-baked slogans of the brutish agitators of the masses. Neither years of schooling and a first-rate pedigree nor simple tastes and a personal knowledge of tough life can immunize us from falling captive to what Plato, in the *Republic*, calls "tyrannical pomp" (577a). If this is the case, then what could comedy possibly offer by way of an antidote to psychological myopia, romanticization of martyrdom, hatred, zealotry, bigotry, isolationism, racism, or some other ugly prosopography of our life?

Laughter avails us of a distance from ourselves and thereby allows us to move closer to the serious self-understanding without which we cannot give due care to our political life. How can we engage in politics and public life thoughtfully if we don't expend much thought in an attempt to know ourselves? In the *Philebus*, Socrates speaks of the "nature of the ridiculous" (*to geloion . . . phusin*, 48c)[15] as a "kind of vice [*ponêria*] that derives its name from a special disposition; it is, among all the vices, the one with a character that stands in direct opposition to the one recommended by the famous inscription in Delphi" (48c). The inscription at the entrance to the temple of the Delphic Apollo commanded: "Know Thyself." Socrates's joke here hinges on the fact that the ridiculous stands in direct opposition to our self-knowledge. Comedy makes use of the downfalls and faults which are ours, but to which we are either purposefully or unknowingly blind. Our quirks, our strong convictions and predilections are funny because we take them too much to heart. We treat them too seriously. Yet, the vice to which Socrates points is vice *only* if we deny ourselves the possibility to laugh at ourselves; to see through the blinding effects of both our good intentions and our problematic habits. There is hardly anyone more laughable than a person who believes that the Delphic inscription can be realized once and for all. One cannot know oneself completely. Comedy and the Delphic injunction work in tandem. The latter is a lifelong exercise that is serious when it is ongoing, and when it seeks but does not claim completion. And comedy is only vicious when it makes light of our flaws while arousing no impetus to reflect on the implications of our limited and finite nature. Of course, in that guise it is no longer comedy, but rather something gratuitously grotesque and even tragic. Because ignorance is the obverse side of knowledge, there is nothing harmful in being laughed at as long as the shame that one feels does not lead to blind anger but to questions.

There is nothing funny about the violence of tyranny. Nonetheless, if we address it through a comedic lens, we are better positioned to ask ourselves difficult and important questions about the destiny of the ideas and beliefs that we hold to be most dear. I regard the concluding discussions of tyranny in the *Republic* as a diagnostic text that reflects back upon the conversations about the Kallipolis and the education of the guardians. It is a text that indicates Plato's critiques of tyrannical inclinations.[16] On this reading, the *Republic* is not so much a manual that offers us political ideals for implementation, but rather a text that treats with levity very serious and very difficult subjects, and thereby helps us identify and perhaps also mitigate the deleterious effects of our own thinking. The next and final section of this chapter discusses several reasons why we can view the *Republic* as a diagnostic text, that is, as a dialogue which serves to show which of our own inclinations may end up causing us to buy into and support tyranny.

The Tyranny Within

Socrates and Adeimantus exchange the speeches that lead up to the discussion of tyranny (558d–562c).[17] Glaucon takes over the conversation at 576b, where the nature of tyranny and tyrannical life is aligned with rule (*gignetai hos an tyrannikôtatos phusei ôn monarchêsê, kai hosô an pleiô chronon en tyrannidi biô*). The preparatory conversation (558–562c) is cast in terms of desire and need. It harkens the reader back to the discussions of the city of needs (369a–371e), the city of pigs (372a–d), and the luxurious or feverish city of relishes (372d–373e) in book II. The last city, given its excessive needs, quickly finds itself at war with its neighbors.

The feverish city is purged, but the threat of war does not cease to haunt the dialogue. It returns with renewed strength when Socrates speaks about the tyrant, who is dead-set on "stirring up war" (567a). Tyranny, which is the fifth and last regime that the interlocutors discuss in the *Republic*, appears to be the rock bottom in terms of politics, psychology, and ethics. The straightforward recap that renders tyranny as an image of the worst kind of life devolves from aristocracy, to "Cretan and Laconian" (544c) regimes (timocracy), through oligarchy, and then democracy, to the "most savage slavery" (564a) of the people under the tyrant. Socrates offers a strict gradation of the political regimes from the best to the worst. The constitutions overlap vertically at the junctures of regime changes, but not horizontally. That is, we do not see much mixing of regimes. Instead, we see a degradation. This is odd, especially since Plato was privy to the violent events of 411 B.C.E. and the later short-lived but no less vicious tyranny of the pro-Spartan oligarchs in 404–403 B.C.E.[18] He was also intimately familiar with the archaic tyrant-kings immortalized in Homer and with Athens's aristocratic tyrants, including those of the pro-democratic variety who were closer to his time.

In the *Gorgias*, for example, Socrates condemns those who think that "harbors and dockyards, walls, and tribute payments and such trash as that" (519a) can make "the city great" (519a). According to Socrates, all these enhancements are adding to the diseased city that "is swollen and festering" (519a). Socrates summarily accuses the older generation of Athenian leaders such as Pericles, Themistocles, Miltiades, and his son, Cimon who, encouraged by his father's victory at Marathon (and if not envious of, then at least attracted to, the riches promised by the lifestyle of the Persian tyrants), engorged Athens with innovations.[19] In so doing, these public figures aimed to ensure their own political power. This is how matters stand in Plato's text. However, even if we grant some of the questionable nature of the alliances that Miltiades[20] had and the political decisions that Themistocles[21] made, or even if we take seriously the rumors about Cimon's dealings with the Macedonian Alexander I,[22] their otherwise illustrious careers hardly deserve to be deemed as simply damaging to Athens. It is even more difficult, though not impossible, to find fault with Pericles.[23] Whether Pericles's Citizenship Law (451 B.C.E.) intended to make Athens great again is unclear. However, it is certain that the law made those who enjoyed the citizenship privileges more powerful and rich. In his law, Pericles introduced an alarming requirement of familial purity and pedigree. The resulting exclusion from the city's political life (among other things) of a number of heretofore qualified individuals yielded the remaining citizens greater authority, political influence, but often also wealth.[24] This is but one practical manifestation of the squarely undemocratic character of ancient Greek life at a time when its political arrangement, in principle, allowed and called for the most direct and widest citizen participation. However, even if we take stock of the faults of the leaders of the Athenian polis, the question remains: Why does Plato have Socrates deliver a diatribe against these historical figures, as if it were true that their actions were unquestionably and unambiguously damaging to Athens?

As a dialogical character, Socrates, at least to some extent, embodies an attitude that he also means to disavow. Socrates's tirade against tyranny can be seen as a tyrannical tirade. This calls us back to the question of self-reflection. What is interesting in the context of Socrates's invective against others is that Socrates, although he calls himself a lover of Alcibiades (*Gorgias* 481d), forgets to reflect on the deleterious effects of his own association with that youth. The Socrates of the dialogues often gives us clues to the limitations and faults of the historical Socrates. No one, not even Socrates, can do total good. He is mortal. Mortals are fallible. Where we do good, we are also liable to do harm. This is the case both for the dialogical characters and for us, ourselves. Fathers are culpable for failing to provide the education that would make their sons truly good (*Meno* 93c–94e). The public leaders are to blame for their failure to educate the population about "justice and self-control" (*Gorgias* 519a). What about the failures of lovers? Socrates is silent about the blame he deserves for falling short in educating his "friend Alcibiades," who in fact will be assassinated when "they [the Athenians] lose not only what they gained but what they had originally as well" (*Gorgias* 519a–b).

In the *Gorgias*, Socrates marks the leaders of Athens, who (with the exception of Themistocles and as far as the list in the *Gorgias* is concerned) themselves come from aristocratic stock, as either being seduced by the riches of tyrants or at least seized by tyrannical kinds of lusts. He is silent about his own case and his questionable influence on Alcibiades. I acknowledge the difference between history and text. However, I wonder about the many-layered accounts that Plato left of Socrates in his dialogues. It is too simple, not to say utterly erroneous, to see Socrates as an altogether salubrious figure who had no hand in exciting the ambitions of his tyrannically minded or morally questionable contemporaries. We do not have to, nor can we, place the blame for the various characters' (e.g., Alcibiades, Phaedrus, Critias, Thrasymachus, Meletus) downfalls squarely on Socrates, but Plato in the dialogues, at least as far as Socrates's character is concerned, gives us reasons to think about Socrates's flirtation with tyranny. To the master eroticist, the beauty of the young sometimes appeared in a ferociously provocative, tyrannical disguise (*Charmides* 155b–e).

The questionable figures of whom Plato knew included some rulers, such as Pisistratus, whom history remembers as tyrannical benefactors of the Athenian demos. In Pisistratus and at least initially (eventually the Alcmaeonids and Pisistratus parted ways), the interests of the aristocracy and the people coincided or, more precisely, through Pisistratus a particular aristocratic family, the Alcmaeonids (Pericles and Alcibiades were Alcmaeonids), found a way to exercise its will over the people. The Alcmaeonids, who had been exiled from Athens after Megacles assassinated Cylon in 632 B.C.E., returned under the archonship of Solon. They gained ascendancy when rule in Athens went to Solon's lover, Pisistratus. Everitt insists that the "Alcmaeonids were not fools. They must have noticed that they and the other great clans lacked popular support. Without it, they would find it hard to hold on to their old monopoly of power. Their best option was to restore Pisistratus and govern through him, be his collective éminence grise."[25] Everitt goes on to say that "despite the family's hostility to tyranny, another Megacles, grandson of the man who massacred the followers of Cylon, did a deal. He would help Pisistratus return to power on condition that he marry his daughter. The aspirant despot agreed,"[26] although Everitt stresses that Pisistratus "already had a perfectly good wife and two healthy sons, Hippias and Hipparchus."[27] Here, I hear historical resonances with Socrates's production, in the *Republic*, of a city that pays especially careful attention to the institution of marriage as a means of maintaining the purity of the guardian race and securing their social status.

Everitt continues: "Pisistratus understood the value of publicity and of symbolism. He staged a grand entrance into Athens. He found an unusually tall young woman from a country district. Pisistratus dressed her up in a suit of armor, taught her how to present herself convincingly as a goddess, and drove her in procession into the city."[28] Everitt relates that "town criers went ahead shouting: 'Men of Athens, give Pisistratus a warm welcome, for Athena herself is bringing him home to her own citadel. She honours him more than all men.' What better way of demonstrating that Pisistratus enjoyed divine approval and had a legitimate claim to rule? Herodotus calls the stunt 'the silliest idea I have ever heard of.'"[29] This could be the inane historical episode that Socrates has in mind when he speaks to Glaucon about the ostentatious and pretentious ways of tyrants, which may very well be "silly" but which hold sway over the public all the same. Although he remains unnamed, the flamboyance of the *Republic*'s tyrant (577a–b) looks a good deal like that of Pisistratus. There are, of course, differences between the historical figure who sought to unify and strengthen Athens, and the dissipated, "drunken, erotic, and melancholic" (573c) tyrant whom Socrates describes. However, let us recall that one of Pisistratus's innovations brought the citizenry together: in "534 B.C.E. . . . [when] Pisistratus, tyrant of Athens, established a new festival . . . in honor of Dionysus Eleuthereus [and] . . . made a contest in tragedy the chief feature of its program."[30] In the *Republic*, Socrates's complaint against the many, who succumb to the blinding effects of the pretentious surface that covers over the twisted ways of tyrannical life, is couched in terms of the props that are used at tragic performances. Socrates pleads with Glaucon that they must find a "man who is not like a child looking from outside and overwhelmed by the tyrannic pomp set up as a façade for those outside, but who rather sees through it adequately" (577a) when the tyrant is "stripped of the tragic gear" (*gymnos an . . . tês tragikês skeuês*, 577b). Pisistratus does not have to be the exact prototype for the tyrant in the *Republic* VIII–IX. However, one of the public works for which history remembers the aristocratically supported Athenian strongman is the formal inauguration of tragic drama, and Socrates's criticism of its effects on the witless public suggests that Pisistratus might well have been on Plato's mind.

We read, furthermore, both in the *Republic* (566b) and in Herodotus's *Histories* (1.59.4), that a tyrant avails himself of the protection of bodyguards. Once Pisistratus had his "club-men," he seized the Acropolis and the Athenian treasury with it. The tyrant of the *Republic*, Socrates tells Adeimantus, "stands in the chariot of the city, now a perfect tyrant instead of a leader" (566d). This line, again, invokes Pisistratus's pompous and even "silly" but effective entrance into Athens with the faux-Athena at his side, and the demos accepts the gloriously accompanied tyrant. The fact that the distance between democracy and tyranny is short is not surprising. Socrates argues for this. However, the historical figure of Pisistratus, who could trace his lineage to Homeric Nestor, not only maintained power over the demos, but also acted tyrannically against the aristocratic elite. If we bring the descriptions of tyranny in books VIII and IX into the shadow of history (history which Plato no doubt knew very well), we realize that *even in the Republic* there is more than a vertical connection between the various regimes.[31] My analysis of the foregoing historical example indicates that the aristocracy was directly involved with tyranny and, through a tyrant, indirectly influenced the politics of the nominally democratic state. However, the tyrant who sought to win favor with the many also put pressure on the wallets of the aristocrats and thus was despised by the elite. In this sense, aristocracy is as likely to support tyranny as to oppose it, depending on whether the particular tyrant has enough cunning to play both sides (i.e., both the common people and the elite). Is the rule of the best over the many exercised tyrannically in the *Republic* as well? I answered this question affirmatively in the preceding chapter, which argued that tyranny underlies the rule of the philosopher-kings.

Now I will establish the relationship between the founding of the best city and the account of the deplorable state in which the polis finds itself under the tyrant in books VIII–IX. Perhaps the most immediate, but not superficial, relationship between the two is the seriousness with which the interlocutors discuss the philosopher-kings and the grave measures to which the tyrant of the concluding books must resort in order to seize power. Socrates tells us that it is necessary to see past the pretended gravitas of the tyrant, but he does not recommend an antidote. Given Socrates's remark that we must learn how to see past the "tragic gear" of the tyrant, I recommend a comedic remedy. If we, like Herodotus, for example, do not fall for a reverent attitude toward a tyrant's ploy but instead see his marvelous displays as a ridiculous substitute for substance, then we are less likely to become inflamed by the tyrant's rhetoric—whether it is the sort that seeks to win us over, or to beat us down and implant fear or the seeds of hatred.

In this way, the *Republic* can be read as an exercise in *maieutics*. Socrates claims this art as one of his expertise. Plato has staged for us a kind of tragicomedy. In it, the interlocutors, won over by Socrates, end up agreeing to the conditions that terminate in but another iteration of tyrannically-bound desire to come out on top. If we blame the tyrant at the end, but do not see how the dialogical events and the roles that the characters played in them lead to and *necessitate* that the dialogue spiral back to tyranny, then we have not been delivered of our own "wind eggs" (*Theaetetus*, 157d). Despite the ostensible structure of the corruption of the regimes, tyranny is not furthest from the best city. Oligarchy is not exempt from tyrants, either, and democracy harbors tyrannical longings and beliefs. Thus we, the citizens of various regimes, should not think that we are immune to tyrannical desires. We would do well by ourselves if we were to admit that there is no panacea against tyranny. Making this admission would help us diagnose the ways in which we may become susceptible to or already have tyrannical views. If seriousness is weaponized at the hands of the tyrant, then it would appear that comedy, satire, and ridicule should be our weapon against tyranny, and even against the various forms of or predilections for tyranny that we might already harbor *within ourselves*. However, to wield such a weapon well means to welcome comedic laughter and not be afraid—every now and again—to end up as the butt of a joke.

The dual nature of Socrates—his gentle and his terrible selves—is not a metaphor for having an epistemological grounding to distinguish the bad from the good. Instead, it is a metaphor for our aesthetic sensibility. As theatergoers we do not have a moral manual or a set of scientific rules that advise us when to feel terrified or saddened. The reason why we laugh at comedy is not because we have unearthed a principle that helps us determine once and for all all instances of laughter. Instead, we laugh at jokes because they are . . . funny. There is an unresolvable ambivalence at the heart of life, which can only be dissected into simple opposites such as "good" and "bad" or "beautiful" and "ugly" at the expense of life. The gravest mistake we can make is to assert that we have situated the decisive difference between these opposites and have established—with incredible precision—what the good is. If we make such an assertion, then we open ourselves immediately to the worst kinds of actions and choices. If we willfully reject the possibility that we might not know what is good in a given situation, then we deny ourselves a chance to think about it, to ask questions, and to reflect. The people who ended up falling for Pisistratus's "silly" stunt took him seriously. They lacked the sensibility that, I propose, we should cultivate in ourselves. The sensibility I have in mind offers no prescriptions or neatly packaged standards, but an ethos—a way of life—that is premised on a capacity to laugh at ourselves and, thereby, to be honest with ourselves.

CONCLUSION

Self-Examination and Communal Justice

In this study of comedy, I have intended to articulate what role it plays in Plato's characters' search for justice in the *Republic*, and with respect to our own lives. Aristophanes's comedies address political problems and aid us in understanding Plato's comedy, thus shedding a new light on Plato's political philosophy. In Plato, comedy sets into motion philosophy's reflection on itself. For us this means that reading Plato's political philosophy, despite the comedic failures of its prescriptions, holds invaluable advice. In shorthand, it states that lacking comedic ridicule and its power to ignite self-reflection, the pursuit of justice inevitably degenerates into the chase after tyranny. Critics of comedy are right to argue that it lessens the gravity of social issues. However, in conclusion, it is not comedy alone, or politics as such, or philosophy, but all three practiced in tandem that lead us to the kind of self-examination which Plato's dialogues hold out as promising a just life.

In Plato's dialogues, the action of the argument moves against its prescriptive statements. The same lines, in effect, argue for and against themselves without canceling out the third argument, which is available not to the dialogical interlocutors, but to the reader. Plato's interlocutors discuss at length psychology, politics, poetry, cosmology, education, nature, and the gods; in short, the things that inscribe the transcendent and the grounding poles of human life. If life is subject to ceaseless transformation that only yields to being captured in yet another movement—of our thought—then it stands to reason that what we wish to glean from Plato's writing—which, as Benardete says, "is an imitation of the trap door in nature"—will show itself more readily if we remain attentive to the protean nature of the dialogues.[1] This nature is best perceived not in any one shape but in metaphoric and metamorphic motion, that is, through the self-undermining and subversive elements of the dialogues, as well as through the convergence of their speciously opposite forms and themes.

Today for us, as for Plato, the question is: What kinds of transformations do persons and nations suffer that allow this malignant growth—tyranny—to arise? It looks as if, when following Plato in an attempt to answer this question, we must refrain from reenacting the tyrannical tendency to authoritarian, finalistic, and dogmatically definitive answers or prescriptions. Instead, engaging Plato's dialogues discursively, and drawing on the self-same dramatic genre (comedy) of which Plato avails himself, this book attempted to tease out several of the ways in which Plato accounts for and thematizes tyranny in the *Republic*. Plato's poetic philosophy does not offer prescriptions, as do manuals and manifestos. It unfolds, like a theatrical performance.[2] The reversal of meaning, which Aristotle's *Poetics* marks as one of the essential components of a good tragedy, and which alters our understanding of the plot (*muthos*), is always under way in Plato's dialogues. If we miss this—if we miss Plato's jokes, and dismiss his mythmaking and poetizing—then we miss out on another foundational dramatic device, which is recognition. To fail to recognize what the reversal of meaning in Plato's dialogical passages indicates is to miss much of Plato's thinking.

The dialogues speak in polyphonic and multidimensional terms. They are tuned to sustain the tension inherent in the power of rhetoric, dialectic, and poetic metaphor, which are able to deliver diametrically opposite conclusions by means of the same passages and procedures. About rhetoric and dialectic, Aristotle argues that it is not by mistake but by their capacity that those two arts can simultaneously entertain contrarily positioned views and eventualities.[3] Hence, to be aware of and to study the contradictions that remain unresolved in the dialogues is not to be mistaken or misled. "The mistake," as I have mentioned to start and worked to explain, "is when you take the details of the dialogue as a constant modification of the themes of the dialogue. But the consequence is that nothing really changes." "Maybe," Benardete recommends, "you always have to do something like what happens in the *Republic*, where you make the move to the invention of the perfect city only in order to step back from it."[4] Following Benardete's advice, I have tried to articulate the contradictory character of many dialogical developments in their iterations of the incongruities of life. I have traced the double character of Plato's arguments where, for example, on the one hand, there is an argument for a philosopher-king, but on the other hand there is a comedic treatment of this same idea, which shows up in the tyrannical side of political elitism. This does not mean that Plato's philosophizing is undone by the self-undermining style of certain dialogical passages. On the contrary, when we begin to think together with and through Plato's subversive writing—instead of retrofitting our lives to some system that may arise out of it, or forcing that writing to substantiate our extant views—then we get a sense of the liberating force of Plato's philosophy. If perceived, it holds out a promise of freedom that can be borne out in life.

The reason why comedy is so important to reading Plato is that it brings to the surface the incongruity in the otherwise convincing presentation of various political ideas. It is true that we must at first take these ideas for what they are. That way, we can tell what sorts of worldviews these ideas support, which sentiments they evoke and perpetuate, and how they might shape our lives were we to adopt them. However, the next move must be to free ourselves from any such demands for application, because as I have shown throughout this book, no such political arrangement which is discussed in the *Republic* is meant prescriptively, but only diagnostically and maieutically. Comedy aids us in this second moment, when we must distance ourselves from what we have understood in order to see these ideas in a new light. Comedy plays up the incongruous elements of neatly inscribed concepts, and by rendering their incoherencies both visible and laughable, it allows us freedom from them. This freedom is a freedom for reflection. We gain interpretive distance not only from the text of the *Republic* and its discussion of politics, but also from ourselves. However, this distance is not the cool stance of a disinterested observer who has no stake in the ideas upon which she reflects. The nature of comedy, especially of Plato's comedy, is such that it draws us in, and what we find to be funny reflects back upon ourselves. Just like the dialogical interlocutors, we discuss policies and best practices in the *Republic* and in life. We pass judgment on various political arrangements both in Plato's text and in our own communities. We give preference to those policies, ideas, and practices that best align with our moral convictions, and possibly also with our opinions about what is good for others and for ourselves. Barring examination, how can we be sure that any such principles and views are sound? It is, then, the virtue of comedy that it often treats very serious realities lightheartedly, allowing us much-needed room to laugh at ourselves. This laughter undermines our self-importance and decenters the privileged position that we lend to our convictions. It takes the sting out of our desire to defend our deep-seated views. This is where comedy becomes most expedient to philosophy, because having taken our guard down, we stand in a better position to examine ourselves. Without such examination, there is no hope for a just life.

NOTES

Introduction

The epigraph for the introduction is a quotation from Seth Benardete, "Second Thoughts," in *Herodotean Inquiries* (South Bend, IN: St. Augustine's Press, 1999), 216.

1. The text that remains definitive on the subject of the philosophical value of Aristophanes's comedies is Leo Strauss's *Socrates and Aristophanes* (Chicago: University of Chicago Press, 1966). Strauss offers a detailed interpretation of Aristophanes's plays, and he discusses their relationship to Plato's dialogues where appropriate. Drew A. Hyland's account of Plato's use of comedy in *Finitude and Transcendence in Platonic Dialogues* (Albany: SUNY Press, 1995) not only detects the affinity between ancient Greek comedy and Plato, but also sets the stage for overcoming—through a recourse to Plato's comedic technique—dogmatic readings of the dialogues (e.g., interpretations that rely on a "Theory of Forms"). A more recent commentary that seeks to articulate both the philosophical and the erotic tenor of Aristophanes's plays, and their place in Plato's thinking, is Bernard Freydberg's *Philosophy and Comedy: Aristophanes, Logos, and Eros* (Bloomington: Indiana University Press, 2008). Sonja Tanner's book *Plato's Laughter: Socrates as a Satyr and Comical Hero* (Albany: SUNY Press, 2017) elucidates Plato's imparting to Socrates a comedic and satirical sensibility. Shane Montgomery Ewegen, in his work entitled *Cratylus: The Comedy of Language* (Bloomington: Indiana University Press, 2013), unearths the humor of that dialogue as well as its philosophical implications.

Plato's concern with politics hardly needs further documenting. Dialogues like the *Laws*, the *Statesman*, and the *Gorgias* continue to shape political thought, and the *Republic* maintains its place as essential reading in political theory. The ancient refractions of Plato's political philosophy (in Aristotle, the Stoics, Cicero, and Plutarch) and the classic English-language commentaries on politics in Plato (Taylor, Rosen, Klein, Strauss, Benardete, Pangle, Barney, Saxonhouse, Nails, Lane) find their match in the interest and conceptual depth that the philosophers who work in the continental school bring to Plato's political ideas (Sallis, Freydberg, Hyland, Howland, Frank, Burger, Kirkland, Sanday, Baracchi, Arruzza). My analysis treads close to these interpretive approaches and also draws (especially for the study of Aristophanes's plays) on the classicists' research (Cornford, Flickinger, Pickard-Cambridge, Haigh, and Vickers).

Chapter 1

1. Michael Vickers, *Aristophanes and Alcibiades: Echoes of Contemporary History in Athenian Comedy* (Berlin: de Gruyter, 2015). Vickers also reports on the retaliation and attacks that those leaders of Athens who were ridiculed in comedies mounted against the playwrights (1). In another text, entitled *Pericles on Stage* (Austin: University of Texas Press, 1997), Vickers relates an incident in which Alcibiades resorted to harsh measures to punish Eupolis's comedic attacks against his persona (xviii). Vickers cites Alcibiades's 415 B.C.E. decree against direct lampooning as the reason for Aristophanes's omission of Alcibiades's name in his *Birds*, for instance. See also Helene P. Foley, who mentions in

"Tragedy and Politics in Aristophanes' *Acharnians*" that it is possible that Cleon brought charges against Aristophanes after the *Knights* (*Journal of Hellenic Studies* 108 [1988]: 33–47, 33n4). See further Thomas A. Dorey's "Aristophanes and Cleon," *Greece & Rome* 3, no. 2 (1956): 132–39.

2. Hyland warns against deriving from the dialogues "Plato's theory of comedy" (*Finitude and Transcendence*, 131). Instead, Hyland urges us to "look . . . closely at the dialogues themselves, at the way comedy arises within them and the way they portray the philosophic life as comic" (131).

3. Zdravko Planinc makes a similar point and cautions both readers and scholars against deriving neat alignments from the structural affinities of Plato's and Aristophanes's plots. See his "Aristophanic Themes in Plato's *Republic*: A Post-Voegelinian Reading," *Political Science Reviewer* 41, no. 1 (2017).

4. Planinc writes of the "misplaced rigor that warms scholars' hearts: either Aristophanes read Plato; or Plato read Aristophanes; or they both read some other common source or sources" (12).

5. See also Aristotle, *Poetics*, trans. Seth Benardete and Michael Davis (South Bend, IN: St. Augustine's Press, 2002). "Story, then, is the first principle and like the soul of tragedy, and characters are second" (1450a39).

6. Hyland, *Finitude and Transcendence*, 130.

7. Hyland, *Finitude and Transcendence*, 130. Meanwhile, Francis M. Cornford in *The Origin of Attic Comedy* (Cambridge: Cambridge University Press, 1934), 71, discusses the four general forms of agon. Among these is the confrontation between youth and old age. The interrogative and probing character of the agon lends itself well to the comedic genre, and as Robert Metcalf (*Philosophy as Agôn: A Study of Plato's Gorgias and Related Texts* [Evanston, IL: Northwestern University Press, 2018]) sees it, is also well suited to the inquisitive and discursive enterprise of philosophy; more specifically, of Plato's dialogues.

8. Unless otherwise indicated, all quotations of the English-language text use Plato, *Republic*, trans. Allan Bloom (New York: Basic Books, 1991). Where the English text differs from Bloom's, the translation is by the author. The ancient Greek-language copy that I use throughout is the Loeb Classical Library edition: *Plato, Republic, Volume I: Books 1–5*, trans. Chris Emlyn-Jones and William Preddy (Cambridge, MA: Harvard University Press, 2013).

9. Marina Berniz McMcoy describes Aristophanic comedy in strikingly similar terms in her book, *Image and Argument in Plato's Republic* (*SUNY Series in Ancient Greek Philosophy*) (Albany: SUNY Press, 2020). I became familiar with McCoy's book after an event on Plato's *Republic* put together by the *Ancient Philosophy Society* on April 20, 2021. In addition to a chapter dedicated to the *Assembly Women* and Kallipolis in her book, McCoy has one other piece on comedy in Aristophanes and Plato's *Protagoras*: an article, "Plato's *Protagoras*, Writing, and the Comedy of Aporia" in *Plato's Protagoras*: *Essays on Confrontation of Philosophy and Sophistry*. Philosophical Studies 125, ed. Olof Pettersson and Vigdis Songe-Møller (Cham, Switzerland: Springer, 2017), 153–64. In her book, McCoy discusses Aristophanes's *Assembly Women* in the context of the Kallipolis. She concludes that Aristophanes's comedy is "neither uncritical nor antirational but rather seeks to reveal the irrational" (156). She then goes on to say that "Aristophanic comedy . . . seeks to affirm democracy by bringing all down to a common level" (156). This conclusion, on my view, goes too far. Comedy, especially philosophically rich comedy, like Aristophanes's, does not seek to equalize us, nor bring everything to a common denominator. For one, excellent

comedy is not accessible to everyone or at least not at all times. One has to be receptive to it both in terms of sensibility and in terms of one's willingness to reflect on the comedic spectacle and its meaning. Furthermore, as I argue in the third chapter of this book, Aristophanes himself compares his art to artful navigation or skillful sailing. Aristophanic comedy is conceptually nuanced and requires a serious commitment on our part in order to be well received and properly understood. In my own published work, I articulate the conceptual value of comedy. I argue that philosophical comedy has the potential to make us aware of our shortcomings and, thereby, to bring us closer to self-examination. I initially developed this idea in my doctoral dissertation, *A Philosophical Study of Tyranny in Plato, Sophocles, and Aristophanes* (defended on May 5, 2017 and made available as a bound printing in fall 2017). Consequently, my conceptualization of the philosophical value of comedy appeared in the following articles: "Plato and Aristophanes on (Want of) Education: Shame and Eros in Plato's *Gorgias* and Aristophanes's *Clouds*," *Ramus: Critical Studies in Greek and Roman Literature* 48 (2) (2019): 127–47; "The Tragedy and Comedy of Tyranny: Plato's *Symposium* and Aristophanes' *Frogs*," *Philosophy and Literature* 44, no. 2 (2020): 207–25; "State Violence and Weaving: Implications of Aristophanes' *Lysistrata* for Plato's *Statesman*," *Journal of Ancient Philosophy* 15, no. 1 (2021), and, of course, throughout this book. All three articles are carefully reworked versions of various parts of my dissertation chapters. However, this book is an entirely new project, which shares some conceptual ideas about comedy with my dissertation but offers entirely new content in terms of the examined dialogue and plays.

10. Mikhail Bakhtin indicates that there is a difference between satire and comedy. Satire leaves the satirist somehow superior to those about whom she jokes. Comedic humor links the joker with her joke, or reflects back unto and includes the comedian as the subject of the joke. See Mikhail Bakhtin, *Rabelais and His World*, trans. Helene Iswolsky (Bloomington: Indiana University Press, 1984), 11–12. See, further, the difference between satire, strictly speaking, and ancient Greek comedy that Freydberg points to in "Hearkening to Thalia: Toward the Rebirth of Comedy in Continental Philosophy," *Research in Phenomenology* 39, no. 3 (2009): 401–15, esp. 402 and 403.

11. Leo Strauss, "The Origins of Political Science and the Problem of Socrates: Six Public Lectures," *Interpretation* 23, no. 2 (Winter 1996): 127–207, 192.

12. Leo Strauss, *Socrates and Aristophanes*, 316n20. See also Claudia Baracchi, who claims that Plato is not reacting, but responding to the Aristophanic Socrates. See Claudia Baracchi, "Beyond the Tragedy and Comedy of Authority," *Philosophy and Rhetoric* 34, no. 2 (2001): 151–76, 153.

13. Seth Benardete, *Encounters and Reflections: Conversations with Seth Benardete*, ed. Ronna Burger (Chicago: University of Chicago Press, 2002), 124.

14. On the subject of the relation between actions and speeches in drama, see Leo Strauss, "The Origins of Political Science and the Problem of Socrates: Six Public Lectures," *Interpretation* 23, no. 2 (Winter 1996): 127–207, 179.

15. Benardete, *Encounters and Reflections*, 125.

16. Renate Schlesier, "Mixtures of Masks: Maenads and Tragic Models," in *Masks of Dionysus*, ed. Thomas H. Carpenter and Christopher A. Faraone (Ithaca, NY: Cornell University Press, 1993), 89–114. My claim about truth and Plato's dialogues stands in direct opposition to what Schlesier writes about the "goals of Plato's thinking" (95). Notwithstanding the disparate conclusions at which we arrive, I agree with Schlesier's insight about truth and reality in their relation to and their multivalent refractions in drama.

17. See Arthur Wallace Pickard-Cambridge, *Dithyramb Tragedy and Comedy* (Oxford: Clarendon, 1927), for a discussion of the initial stages of ancient Greek drama and the introduction of the practice of masking the actors' faces (111–12). See also Carpenter and Faraone, *Masks of Dionysus*, for the sources that discuss the mask in relation to Dionysus (2–3). See, finally, Roy C. Flickinger, *The Greek Theater and Its Drama* (Chicago: University of Chicago Press, 1936), for a discussion of the relationship between the worship of Dionysus in Greece and ancient Greek dramatic performances (119–24).

18. See Schlesier, "Mixtures of Masks," 95n27.

19. Benardete, *Encounters and Reflections*, 124.

20. Schlesier, "Mixtures of Masks," examines ancient Greek drama and says that "the 'visual meaning' of Greek drama sometimes implies the transformation of words heard into a vision" (95n27).

21. Benardete, *Encounters and Reflections*, 124.

22. Hyland, *Finitude and Transcendence*, 89.

23. Hyland, *Finitude and Transcendence*, 110.

24. Pickard-Cambridge, *Dithyramb Tragedy and Comedy*, 144. Pickard-Cambridge gives several appendixes that treat the different theories of the beginning, origin, and form of ancient Greek comedy.

25. Pickard-Cambridge, *Dithyramb Tragedy and Comedy*, 145.

26. Pickard-Cambridge, *Dithyramb Tragedy and Comedy*, 144.

27. Pickard-Cambridge, *Dithyramb Tragedy and Comedy*, 225–26.

28. Aristotle, *Poetics*, 1448a28–29.

29. Aristotle, *Poetics*, 1448a27–28.

30. Aristotle, *Poetics*, 1448a30–31.

31. Aristotle, *Poetics*, 1448a36–1448b.

32. Flickinger, *The Greek Theater and Its Drama*, 36. On the origin of comedy and the relationship between satyr plays, phallic processions, Dionysus, and comedy, see Rebecca Lämmle, *Poetik des Satyrspiels* (Heidelberg: Universitätsverlag, 2013). See also Pickard-Cambridge's description of the bawdy, Silenic nature of Aristophanes's comedy. About the *Birds*, he writes that the "masks, which the actors wear in Aristophanes' plays, at once exaggerate and variegate the attitudes that the comedic characters exhibit. Whereas it is probable that the members of a tragic chorus were all masked alike, this was not always so in comedy, for example, in the *Birds* (268–304)" (Pickard-Cambridge, *The Dramatic Festivals of Athens* [Oxford: Oxford University Press, 1968], 195). He continues: "All kinds of birds are represented in the chorus. How the choruses which represented ordinary human beings were masked there is no precise evidence to show, but old men and women were doubtless rendered grotesque in some way" (195).

33. Flickinger, *The Greek Theater and Its Drama*, 36.

34. Flickinger, *The Greek Theater and Its Drama*, 36.

35. Flickinger, *The Greek Theater and Its Drama*, 36.

36. In *Philosophy and Comedy*, Freydberg situates the characters of Aristophanes's comedies and Plato's Socratic comedy under the aegis of Dionysus and Apollo, respectively. However, I trace out a much closer proximity between Plato's and Aristophanes's comedic genre and claim that both the plays and the dialogues offer the sorts of scenes, utterances, and actions that fall under the auspices of Dionysian—that is, bawdy, raucous, and even vulgar—comedy.

37. Flickinger, *The Greek Theater and Its Drama*, 21. Flickinger's discussion of the development of tragedy out of the dithyrambic songs to Dionysus is also helpful.

38. The dramatic performances were held twice a year; once in the early spring, at the City Dionysia in Athens, which was the "last of the Athenian festivals of Dionysus to be instituted" (Pickard-Cambridge, *The Dramatic Festivals of Athens*, 92); and once more, January–February, at the Lenaion sanctuary. Thus, the smaller, rural Dionysian celebration is known by the name of the Lenaean Dionysia. The winter dithyrambic performances marked the three months sacred to Dionysus and drew, to Delphi, the embassies of *theôriai*—the reverent visitations from Athens. The great City Dionysia, held in March and April, was the only festival named after the Olympian in whose honor it was celebrated. Susan G. Cole ("Under the Open Sky: Imagining the Dionysian Landscape," in *Human Developments in Sacred Landscapes*, ed. Lutz Kappel and Vassiliki Pothou [Gottingen: V&R Unipress, 2015]) tells us that the "Dionysia could not begin until a *xoanon* (a small portable wooden image of the divinity) was carried to the city center from Eleutherai on the Boeotian border" (63). Cole goes on to describe the festival in her "Procession and Celebration at the Dionysia," in *Theater and Society in the Classical World*, ed. Ruth Scodel (Ann Arbor: University of Michigan Press, 1993). "The wooden statue was installed at the *eschara*, or hearth, in a sanctuary of Dionysus near the Academy, from which it was carried in an evening procession, lit by torches, to the sanctuary of Dionysus Eleuthereus near the theater in the center of the city. The climax of this evening ceremony was the sacrifice of the bull" (27). These annual ritualistic celebrations commemorated the arrival of Dionysus, who had originally come to Attica from Boeotia when the citizens of the town of Eleutherae brought the statue of Dionysus to Athens. The Athenians, who at first rejected the statue, suffered a calamity—a disease that affected male genitalia. Cole says that the "disease stopped only when the Athenians honored the god by making phalloi, both at public and at private expense. The myth," Cole goes on, "is only a crude etiology for the ritual of the phallerophoria, but it shows that the phalloi were carried to offer honor (τιμή) [*timê*] to the god and to avoid his anger" (26). Though initially revered in the countryside and overseen by the *archon* (seventh century B.C.E.), sometime in the sixth century B.C.E., the Dionysian revelry and the mysteries connected with Dionysus—the spectacles beholden to the god—overflowed into the celebrations of dramatic theatrical performances. The contemplation of a god was transformed into and connected to the act of spectatorship. Both divinity and drama informed the ancient Greek practice of reflection, and so there is a proximity for us, too, between contemplation (*theaomai*), theater (*theatron*), and theory (*theôrein*). Pickard-Cambridge writes on the subject that

> it is impossible to trace in detail the route or routes by which the worship of Dionysus . . . reached Athens. Dionysus was certainly a god of the Thraco-Phrygian stock, and it is probable that he was worshiped both in Thrace and in Asia Minor. . . . There is little doubt that Delphi assisted in propagation. There are legends of his reception at Icaria, at Acharnae and at Eleutherae; and while an elementary form of drama . . . was the foundation of the tragedy of Thespis, the worship of the god in the Peloponnese . . . contributed, in all probability, the higher lyric elements which found a place in tragedy, and also the satyr-play which was brought into Athens from Phlius. (Pickard-Cambridge, *Dithyramb Tragedy and Comedy*, 174).

Consider, also, Richard Seaford's observation that "Dionysus [is] almost entirely absent from Homer" in "Dionysus as Destroyer of the Household: Homer, Tragedy, and the Polis," in *Masks of Dionysus*, ed. Thomas H. Carpenter and Christopher A. Faraone (Ithaca, NY: Cornell University Press, 1993), 142.

39. Vickers, *Pericles on Stage*, xv.

40. Cleon, whom the character of the Paphlagonian tanner is supposed to represent in Aristophanes's *Knights*, although himself of aristocratic heritage, rose to power in Athens by winning favor with and promoting the interests of the commercial class. Themistocles, who is often recognized in one of the slaves or servants of Demos, was not an aristocrat and rose to power largely by catering to the needs of the demos. See Mabel Lang, "Cleon as the Anti-Pericles," *Classical Philology* 67, no. 3 (1927): 159–69. Lang discusses the respective positions that Cleon, Themistocles, and Pericles held with regard to the Athenian demos.

41. See Jacob Howland, *Glaucon's Fate: History, Myth, and Character in Plato's Republic* (Philadelphia: Paul Dry Books, 2018). Howland offers examples of historical anachronisms in the *Parmenides*, *Symposium*, *Menexenus*, and the *Republic*. This does not mean that "Plato is unconcerned with history," but "like myth, the story"—the narrative arc of Plato's dialogues—"develops independently of historical time" (33).

42. Strauss, "The Origins of Political Science," 180.

43. Strauss, "The Origins of Political Science," 180.

44. Jacques Derrida urges us to "observe that reading proceeds in no other way. It listens in watching." See Derrida's *Memoirs of the Blind: The Self-Portrait and Other Ruins*, trans. Pascale-Anne Brault and Michael Naas (Chicago: University of Chicago Press, 1993), 2.

45. Strauss, "The Origins of Political Science," 202.

46. Hyland, *Finitude and Transcendence*, 169.

47. Bernard Freydberg, *The Play of the Platonic Dialogues: Literature and the Sciences of Man* (New York: Peter Lang, 1997).

48. In *The Play of the Platonic Dialogues*, Freydberg refers to the "dense two pages" in which "Sallis declares play to be nothing less than the appropriate entrance to philosophy, and its appropriate practice" (4).

49. John Sallis, *Being and Logos: Reading the Platonic Dialogues* (Bloomington: Indiana University Press, 1975), 312.

50. John Sallis, *Being and Logos*, 21n12.

51. Sallis, *Being and Logos*.

52. See Sallis, "Logos and Its Parts: *Cratylus*," in *Being and Logos*, and in particular, 217–62.

53. See Seth Benardete, *The Tragedy and Comedy of Life: Plato's Philebus* (Chicago: University of Chicago Press, 1993). On Plato's use of comedic language, characters, and scenes, see William Chase Greene, "The Spirit of Comedy in Plato," *Harvard Studies in Classical Philology* 31 (1920): 63–123.

54. Seth Benardete, *The Argument in the Action* (Chicago: University of Chicago Press, 2000), 175.

55. Freydberg comments on the passage about communal naked exercises and asks whether "deliberation [could] produce a more ridiculous result" (*Philosophy and Comedy*, 121).

56. On the question of inhumanity and tyranny in the *Symposium* and in the historical Athens in fourth century B.C.E., see Marina Marren, "The Tragedy and Comedy of Tyranny: Plato's *Symposium* and Aristophanes' *Frogs*," *Philosophy and Literature* 44, no. 2 (2020): 207–25. See further Marren's "Ascent to Αὐτὸ τὸ Καλόν in Plato's *Symposium* 204a–212d" in *Looking at Beauty to Kalon in Western Greece*, ed. L. Reid and Tony Leyh (Sioux City, IA: Parnassos Press, 2019), 133–48.

57. Benardete, *The Argument in the Action*, 172–75.

58. A tragic reading of the *Republic*, I contend, is not the same as a reading of the dialogue as if it were a tragedy.

59. Notably, at line 506d in the *Republic*, with the words: "You're not going to withdraw when you are, as it were, at the end," Glaucon takes over the conversation that Socrates was having with Adeimantus. Glaucon's and Socrates's previous conversation had ended with Glaucon's agreement that rule in the city should be secured for the one who is "by nature a rememberer, a good learner, magnificent, charming, and a friend and kinsman of truth, justice, courage, and moderation" (*Republic* 487a). Benardete's explanation of the function of the ascent to the Good supports the idea that if it is read straightforwardly, it remains misunderstood. He writes that the "sixth and seventh books bear to Socratic philosophizing the same relation the city in speech bore to the dialogic city. They represent this rival account of philosophy and at the same time contain Socrates' refutation of it." See his *The Second Sailing: On Plato's Republic* (Chicago: University of Chicago Press, 1989), 140.

60. Howland, *Glaucon's Fate*, esp. 6–16 and 54. On the subject of Glaucon's eroticism, see Stanley Rosen, who observes that there is a peculiar overabundance of erotic and generative language in the "ascent to the Good" passages. See Rosen, "The Role of Eros in Plato's *Republic*," *Review of Metaphysics* 18, no. 3 (1965): 452–75, esp. 472–74.

61. See Michael Davis, *The Poetry of Philosophy* (South Bend, IN: St. Augustine's Press, 1992), 39–40.

62. See Ronna Burger's discussion of the relationship between pleasure and the good in *Aristotle's Dialogue with Socrates: On the Nicomachean Ethics* (Chicago: University of Chicago Press, 2008), 154–58. See also Benardete's conclusions about pleasure and self-aware thinking in "Aristotle, 'De Anima' III.3–5," *Review of Metaphysics* 28, no. 4 (1975): 611–22.

63. Howland observes that it is nothing other than "Gygean pleasures and honors that make Glaucon extremely eager to know how to bring the regime into being." See his "Glaucon's Fate: Plato's *Republic* and the Drama of the Soul," *Proceedings of the Boston Area Colloquium for Ancient Philosophy* 29, no. 1 (2014): 113–46, 114. See also Howland, *Glaucon's Fate*, 13.

In the context of Socrates's conversations with and influence on his younger, power-hungry or self-centered interlocutors, consider Benardete's remarks about Lysis in *The Argument of the Action*. Benardete notes that "it is through wisdom, Socrates tells Lysis, that Lysis could be universally loved and at the same time gain the freedom to do as he liked" (199). This describes Glaucon equally well. Giving yet another description of Glaucon and his misunderstanding of the dialogical developments, Benardete writes in *The Second Sailing*: "Glaucon's demand that the good city in speech be realized measures exactly the degree to which he has not understood the *Republic*. That he speaks of the regime's feasibility and not the city's, shows that he has in mind the transformation of an actual city (471c7, e2)" (123). Later on, in the same work, Benardete describes Glaucon's lack of understanding in view of what the reader is meant to glean from his shortsightedness. "We have the measure of the difference between the *Republic* and the movement of *logos* itself when we consider that Socrates will prove to Glaucon that the just man is happy without ever showing him even his opinion of the good (533a1–7)." Benardete continues: "Glaucon will be satisfied before it is reasonable for him to be convinced that the rulers of the city he helped to found can know what Socrates says is indispensable if they are to rule. The good for Glaucon is as fragmentary as his understanding, but all the same it is complete" (171). Benardete concludes that "it is this notion of the good as good for something that is missing from Socrates' description of intellection. It is *logos* without the soul that moves so easily from start to finish" (171). And again, later, in relation to the ascent from the Cave, Benardete suggests that "it was Glaucon, then, who in his objection to Socrates's refutation of Thrasymachus, had stopped in his ascent from the cave at the artifacts outside the wall and mistaken them for the real and his own liberation as complete. Glaucon had taken the prevailing opinion about justice and brought it to the highest degree of Thrasymachean precision" (178–79). Glaucon, Benardete goes on, "claimed that it was an image of justice itself and asked Socrates to dispute about that intentional image as if it were the real thing. Glaucon had presented the impossible as the image of the truly real, and Socrates was to prove that a lifeless being was happy and the wholly imaginary was good" (178–79).

64. Debra Nails, *The People of Plato: A Prosopography of Plato and Other Socratics* (Indianapolis: Hackett, 2002), 115.

65. Benardete, *The Argument of the Action*, 380.

66. Benardete, *Encounters and Reflections*, 130.

67. Howland's interpretation offers a direct link between Glaucon's character and tyranny when he writes that "the internal evidence of the *Republic* . . . all points in the same direction: Glaucon actively supported the Thirty, and most likely met his end at Munychia, somewhere near the place where a group from the Piraeus stops his ascent to Athens in the dialogue's opening scene. If I am right," Howland continues, "Plato's first readers would naturally have regarded the dialogue as a high-stakes philosophical drama—the tragedy of Socrates' unsuccessful struggle to save Glaucon from the corrupting influence of his family and his city" (Howland, "Glaucon's Fate," 113). See also Benardete's discussion of tyranny and "political life" (*Encounters and Reflections*, 132).

68. See Howland, *Glaucon's Fate*, for his take on the licentious promises of the Kallipolis (49).

69. Stanley Rosen, *Plato's Republic: A Study* (New Haven, CT: Yale University Press, 2005), 62.

70. Xenophon, *Memorabilia*, trans. Amy L. Bonnette (Ithaca, NY: Cornell University Press, 1994), 3.6.

71. Rosen, *Plato's Republic*, 80.

72. The word translated as "relish" is *opson*, which designates a cooked item. This word "*opson*" is very close—at least phonetically—to *opsis*, which is a term that means "appearance," but also "sight." For this close correspondence between sights and pleasantries or relishes, see, for example, book 6.24.3 of Thucydides, *The History of the Peloponnesian War*, *The Landmark Thucydides: A Comprehensive Guide to the Peloponnesian War*, trans. Richard Crawley, ed. Robert B. Strassler (New York: Touchstone, 2013). This linguistic play and proximity become important when Socrates introduces the second-order relishes into the feverish city; such things as beauticians, for example, who have to do, precisely, with making one more pleasing to the eye, but also poets and actors whose works are spectacles (373a–c). The verb form of *opson* is *epsô*, that is, "to boil." The *Greek-English Lexicon* confirms the sense of *opson* as a "cooked or otherwise prepared dish." See *Greek-English Lexicon*, ed. Henry George Liddell and Robert Scott (Oxford: Clarendon, 1953), 1283. In the immediately following discussion at *Republic* 373b–c, the term *opson* introduces the "city . . . gorged with a bulky mass of things [and with] . . . need of . . . relish-makers and

cooks" (*opsopoiôn te kai mageirôn*). Note, also, that when Glaucon launches his complaint against the unadorned simplicity of the city, he is especially concerned about the fate of men. The term that Glaucon uses at 372c is "*andras*," which is a plural of *anêr*, not of the generic "*anthrôpos*."

73. Compare this point, at which the construction of the *huôn polin* or "city of pigs" begins, to the point of the promised finish line in the *Statesman*, which is reached by the slowest things that arrive last, *hustata aphiknesthai ta bradutata* (266c). See also Benardete's note on the *Statesman* passage, "the word for 'last' (*hustaton*) puns on the word for 'pig' (*hus*)." This remark appears in *The Being of the Beautiful: Plato's Theaetetus, Sophist, and Statesman*, trans. Seth Benardete (Chicago: University of Chicago Press, 2006), III.151n14.

74. Lämmle, *Poetik des Satyrspiels*, 271. Translation by the author.

75. I am referring to the passage from Homer's *Odyssey* in which Odysseus's companions, by means of Circe's magic, are made to look like pigs, while "their human sense was unaltered." The line appears in book X.240, Homer, *Odyssey*, trans. Brian Kemball-Cook (New York: Calliope, 1993). The question is, of course, whether Circe's magic should be seen as capable of masking or, rather, revealing the true appearances of things.

76. It is rather the case that the "bestialization of man belongs together with the civilization of man," as Benardete observes in *The Argument of the Action* (194).

77. Liddell and Scott, *Greek-English Lexicon*, 322. Kenneth J. Reckford further remarks about Aristophanes's *Assembly Women* that it offers "abundance and ease," but at the fair price of one's humanity, because the men, according to Praxagora's plan, will be fed like cattle. Reckford observes that "Praxagora's word for it [is] . . . *boskēsomai*." See Reckford, *Aristophanes' Old-and-New Comedy, Volume I: Six Essays in Perspective* (Chapel Hill: University of North Carolina Press, 2010), 351. This is the same word that Socrates uses to refer to the feeding practices in the luxurious city of book II. Reckford also compares Praxagora's fattened men to Circe's pigs in the *Odyssey*.

78. Howland, too, attributes to Glaucon a desire for honor, which can be appeased in competitions and in war. Since both are absent from the simple city, Glaucon finds such a city to be wanting (*Glaucon's Fate*, 56–62).

79. My understanding of "sublimation" is informed by Sigmund Freud's meaning. See his *Das Unbehagen in der Kultur* (Berlin: Europäischer Literaturverlag, 2015), 21–22, and note 8 on page 22.

80. Hyland, *Finitude and Transcendence*, 130. In addition to Hyland's understanding of the relationship between the comedic and the dialogical agon, see also Metcalf, *Philosophy as Agôn*.

81. Howland sees Socrates as someone who "excites" Glaucon "by giving him cause to imagine that, in Callipolis, he could be not just an acclaimed warrior, enjoying the Homeric excess of food, sex, violence, and honor with which the regime rewards its most disciplined and courageous combatants, but perhaps even a philosopher-king" (*Glaucon's Fate*, 11).

82. By "purification" I also mean a kind of sublimation where the so-called "base" desire for pleasure gets expressed as the desire for the pleasures that are "good."

83. As Howland puts it, "one must also reckon with the historical legacy of the view that Callipolis is not just Plato's vision of the best regime, but what is more, a positive recommendation for political action. The first step in this reckoning is to show . . . that this interpretation involves a fundamental misunderstanding of the dialogue" (*Glaucon's Fate*, 21).

84. Especially the interpretations of Ulrich von Wilamowitz, *Platon* (Berlin: Weidmann, 1917); Werner Jaeger, *Paideia: Die Formung des griechischen Menschen* (Berlin: de Gruyter, 1933); and Kurt Hildebrandt, *Platon. Der Kampf des Geistes um die Macht* (Berlin: Georg Bondi, 1933).

85. Sallis, *Being and Logos*, 312.

86. Sallis, *Being and Logos*, 316.

87. Benardete, *Encounters and Reflections*, 128–34.

88. See Freydberg, *The Play of the Platonic Dialogues*, 11–65. Consider also the tragicomic implications suggested by Freydberg's analysis of the *Republic*'s many cities (82–83).

Chapter 2

1. Walter Burkert, *Homo Necans: The Anthropology of Ancient Greek Sacrificial Ritual and Myth*, trans. Peter Bing (Berkeley: University of California Press, 1983), 143–49. See also Jennifer Larson, whose account of the sorts of things that women and girls carried in their festive baskets during the nighttime procession of Scirophoria suggests comedic undertones. See Larson's *Ancient Greek Cults* (New York: Routledge, 2007), 45–46.

2. Howland points out that in its first lines, the *Republic* invokes a *theoric* practice—spectatorship or observation of the spectacle dedicated to Bendis (*Glaucon's Fate*, 34–35).

3. Sallis connects the mention of the Panathenaea with Athenian victories over Persia. He observes that the "Panathenaea was primarily a celebration of the Athenian victories by land and sea in the Persian wars, the wars in which Persia sought to expand into the eastern Mediterranean by subjugating the Greek cities." See also Sallis's *Chorology: On Beginning in Plato's Timaeus* (Bloomington: Indiana University Press, 1999), 41. Proclus makes a comparison between the greater and the lesser Panathenaea. According to him, "we can survey the difference between the *Parmenides* and this dialogue [the *Timaeus*]. For both have their hypothesis in the Panathenaea; but the former in the greater, and the latter in the lesser of these solemnities. For they were celebrated about the same time with the Bendidian festival." Proclus further observes that the festival is "said to have been celebrated in the Piraeus. . . . But that the Panathenaean followed the Bendidian festivals is asserted." See Proclus, *The Commentaries of Proclus on the Timaeus of Plato, in Five Books; Containing a Treasury of Pythagoric and Platonic Physiology*, trans. Thomas Taylor (London: A. J. Valpy, Red Lion Court, 1820), 62–63.

4. Larson, *Ancient Greek Cults*, 46–47. See also Charles Waldstein's careful research on the Panathenaic festival in "The Panathenaic Festival and the Central Slab of the Parthenon Frieze," *American Journal of Archaeology and of the History of the Fine Arts* 1, no. 1 (1885): 10–17. See also the digitized entry on "Panathenaea," in *A Dictionary of Greek and Roman Antiquities*, ed. William Smith, William Wayte, and G. E. Marindin (London: John Murray, 1890), at http://www.perseus.tufts.edu.

5. Anthony Everitt informs us about the peplos weaving rituals that accompanied the greater Panathenaea. Note that weaving is a trope in Homer (e.g., Penelope's weaving) and it also features as a metaphor for rule throughout the second half of Plato's *Statesman*. Weaving is Lysistrata's violent solution to the perils of war in Aristophanes's eponymous play. Everitt further mentions that the "quadrennial festival in honor of the goddess [Athena]" included "poetry and music contests, introduced by Pericles." See his *The Rise of Athens: The Story of the World's Greatest Civilization* (New York: Random House, 2016), 263. "The first four days of the festival," Everitt goes on to say, "were open to foreigners, but the fifth was restricted to the ten Athenian Tribes. A popular event was a male beauty

contest, the *euandria*, in which the tribes competed for a generous prize of 100 drachmas and an ox."

6. Peter Londey, who relies on Plutarch's account, problematizes the possible motives and outcomes of this mission. See Londey's "Perikles vs Thrace, 447 BC," in *Eleventh International Congress of Thracology* (proceedings from conference held in Istanbul, November 8–12, 2010), ed. Mustafa H. Sayar (2016), 159–64.

7. Jacob Burckhardt, *The Greeks and Greek Civilization*, trans. Sheila Stern and ed. Oswyn Murray (New York: St. Martin's Griffin Press), 227. See also Donald Kagan, *The Peace of Nicias and the Sicilian Expedition: A New History of the Peloponnesian War* (Ithaca, NY: Cornell University Press, 1991), 157; Plutarch, Plutarch: Lives, vol. 3, Pericles and Fabius Maximus, Nicias and Crassus, trans. Bernadotte Perrin (Cambridge, MA: Harvard University Press, 1916), 2.5.

8. "Periclean Imperial Policy and the Mytelenean Debate," *Acta Classica* 6 (1963): 106–24, 111.

9. "Periclean Imperial Policy and the Mytelenean Debate," *Acta Classica* 6 (1963): 106–24, 111

10. *The Athenian Empire* (New York: Charles Scribner's Sons, 1887), 41.

11. Petra Janouchová, "The Cult of Bendis in Athens and Thrace," *Graeco-Latina Brunensia* 18, no. 1 (2013): 95–106. See also Beth Cohen, ed., *Not the Classical Ideal: Athens and the Construction of Other in Greek Art* (Leiden: Brill, 2000), 364–92; and Larson, *Ancient Greek Cults*, 179–177.

12. Janouchová, "The Cult of Bendis," 106; Thucydides, *The History of the Peloponnesian War*, 2.29.

13. Janouchová confirms that the "reason for such a major change in Athenian religion was however not religious, but rather political: as mentioned above, the act was an ultimate diplomatic concession in order to win the favour and resources of the Thracian king" ("The Cult of Bendis," 96).

14. The foreign hunter goddess Bendis, which was then new to Athens, whom the Bendideia festival celebrated, is depicted on a *skyphos* held at the Tübingen University Museum. The artifact is thought to commemorate the events of the Bendideian festivities. Here is how the exhibit plate adjacent to the *skyphos* (430–425 B.C.E.) describes the depicted event:

> A: Themis, the embodiment of the divine law, holding the sacrificial basket (*kanoun*) and the torch, greets Bendis, the Thracian goddess. Bendis, who is led by the deer, is recognizable as Artemis, the huntress, by her double-girdled short chiton, boots, and lances. She is also wearing a doeskin and a fox fur cap.
>
> B: Artemis, clad in huntress attire, is standing by the hunter Kephalos who, sitting down by the ithyphallic Herm, offers a libation. His dog, Laelaps, is sniffing a hedgehog.
>
> The cult of the Thracian goddess Bendis in Athens, in the year 430/429 B.C.E. was elevated to the rank of a state cult. In the introduction to the *Republic*, Plato describes the first festival in celebration of the Bendideia in Piraeus, [which took place] near the Artemis temple in Munychia. Socrates and his friends were then drawn to Piraeus to honor and worship the new goddess as well as to see the [joint] procession of the Thracians and the Athenians. Prior to the nocturnal part of the festivities, marked by horseback torch races that were heretofore

> unknown in Athens, Socrates stopped by the [house of] Polemarchus, Cephalus's [Kephalos's] son.
>
> The historical aspect of the vase's production is hardly confirmed by this extravagant *skyphos*. Was the mythical Cephalus included in the representation because the order [to make the vase] came from the house of the historical Cephalus? And what was the vase painter thinking as he placed a hedgehog right under the nose of the unsurpassably swift dog Laelaps whom no game, except for the uncatchable Theumessian fox, could escape? (Translation from the German is by the author.)

The ancient Greek inscription at the bottom of the plate reads:

ΚΕΦΑΛΟΣ | ΑΡΤΕΜΙΣ | ΘΕΜΙΣ | ΒΕΝ

The hedgehog, placed near Laelaps, is an ancient Egyptian symbol of rebirth (winter hibernation and return to active life in the spring). The animal is also associated with Ishtar, the Babylonian goddess of love and war.

15. Freydberg, *Philosophy and Comedy*, 118. See also the passages about dye in the *Republic* (429c–430b). See, further, Freydberg's take on references to innovation in the play. Moreover, Reckford in *Aristophanes' Old-and-New Comedy*, thinks that at the time and in the Athenian political "context . . . the joke [about innovation] seems painful" (346).

16. Strauss, *Socrates and Aristophanes*, 269.

17. Strauss, *Socrates and Aristophanes*, 269.

18. Julius Moravcsik, "Inner Harmony and the Human Ideal in *Republic* IV and IX," *Journal of Ethics* 5, no. 1 (2001): 39–56; Richard D. Parry, *Plato's Craft of Justice* (Albany: SUNY Press, 1996).

19. J. R. S. Wilson, "The Argument of *Republic* IV," *Philosophical Quarterly* 26, no. 103 (1976): 111–24; Gregory Vlastos, *Platonic Studies* (Princeton, NJ: Princeton University Press, 1973), 130. Vlastos's analysis was also published in a slightly different form in *Plato: A Collection of Critical Essays 2*, ed. Gregory Vlastos (New York: Anchor Books, 1971).

20. William W. Fortenbaugh, "On Plato's Feminism in 'Republic' V," *Apeiron: A Journal for Ancient Philosophy and Science* 9, no. 2 (1975): 1–4.

21. Christine Pierce, "Equality: 'Republic' V," *The Monist*, "Women's Liberation: Ethical, Social, and Political Issue," vol. 57, no. 1 (1973): 1–11.

22. Sara Brill, *Plato on the Limits of Human Life* (Bloomington: Indiana University Press, 2013), 105.

23. Cinzia Arruzza, "The Private and the Common in Plato's 'Republic,'" *History of Political Thought* 32, no. 2 (2011): 215–33.

24. See Nikos G. Charalabopoulos, who argues that Plato's dialogues are steeped in the theatrical tradition and serve as a substitute, of sorts, for the performances of drama. See his *Platonic Drama and Its Ancient Reception* (Cambridge: Cambridge University Press, 2012). On Plato and theater, see also Ruby Blondell, *The Play of Character in Plato's Dialogues* (Cambridge: Cambridge University Press, 2006). On the subject of comedy in general, and more specifically, on the relationship between Aristophanes's plays and Plato, see Freydberg, *Philosophy and Comedy*; Strauss, *Socrates and Aristophanes*; Strauss, "The Origins of Political Science" (1996); Hyland, *Finitude and Transcendence*; and Richard Patterson, "The Platonic Art of Comedy and Tragedy," *Philosophy and Literature* 6, no. 1 (1982): 76–93. See an analysis of Plato's dialogues as works of drama in Catherine H. Zuckert, "Is There a 'Straussian' Plato?" *Review of Politics* 74 (2012): 109–26; and

see also Debra Nails, "Tragedy Off-Stage," in *Plato's Symposium: Issues in Interpretation and Reception*, ed. Jim H. Lesher, Debra Nails, and Frisbee C. C. Sheffield (Cambridge, MA: Harvard University Press, 2006). On drama in Plato, see also Blondell, *The Play of Character*; Freydberg, *The Play of the Platonic Dialogues*; Sallis, *Being and Logos*; James Arieti, *Interpreting Plato: The Dialogues as Drama* (Lanham, MD: Rowman and Littlefield, 1991); Henry G. Wolz "Philosophy as Drama: An Approach to Plato's Dialogues," *International Philosophical Quarterly* 3, no. 2 (1936): 236–70; and Henry G. Wolz, "Philosophy as Drama: An Approach to Plato's *Symposium*," *Philosophy and Phenomenological Research* 30, no. 3 (1970): 323–53.

25. Hunter Ellis, "The *Ecclesiazusae* and the *Republic*," *International Journal of the Humanities: Annual Review* 9, no. 1 (2011): 177–86.

26. Ellis, "The *Ecclesiazusae* and the *Republic*," 177. See also Strauss, *Socrates and Aristophanes*, 264.

27. See both Arlene Saxonhouse, "Comedy in the Callipolis: Animal Imagery in the *Republic*," *American Political Science Review* 72, no. 3 (1978): 888–901, 891n8; and Ellis, "The *Ecclesiazusae* and the *Republic*," 177n3, for a list of authors who argue for linguistic and conceptual parallels between the *Ecclesiazusae* and the *Republic*.

28. Aristophanes, *Aristophanes: Lysistrata, Thesmophoriazusae, Ecclesiazusae, Plutus*, trans. Benjamin Bickley Rogers (Cambridge, MA: Harvard University Press, 1986). I use this English-language translation of the *Ecclesiazusae*. Where the English text differs from Loeb, the translation is by the author.

29. Freydberg sees in Praxagora a woman interested in justice (*Philosophy and Comedy*, 111–57). In another essay, Freydberg stresses the affinity between Aristophanes's and Socrates's eros for justice ("Hearkening to Thalia," 401–15). As Freydberg understands it, such an eros points toward the philosophical dimension of both Platonic and Aristophanic comedy.

30. See Freydberg, *Philosophy and Comedy*. He points out that at the trial run of their presentation at the assembly, one of the women botches her image and her speech. The reason why she does so is because she looks and speaks like a man, that is, like a "garlanded drunkard" (117). This image is reminiscent of the closing scene in Plato's *Symposium*, where none other but Alcibiades appears drunk and garlanded. Praxagora's admonishment of a woman who acts like a lunatic is Aristophanes's jab against leaders like Alcibiades, who brought Athens to its knees.

31. Casement goes as far as to suppose that all of book V is meant seriously, at least by Plato. He claims that "Aristophanes is not an advocate of the Utopian ideas he presents, whereas Plato means to support his." See William Casement, "Political Theory in Aristophanes' *Ecclesiazusae*," *Journal of Thought* 21, no. 4 (1986): 64–79, esp. 68.

32. Laude Mossé, *Athens in Decline, 404–86 B.C.* (Abingdon-on-Thames, UK: Routledge, 1973), 21–49, esp. 24. Compare Mossé's assessment of Athens to Reckford's take on the state of politics in Athens at the time of Aristophanes's play (*Aristophanes' Old-and-New Comedy*, esp. 344).

33. Casement, "Political Theory in Aristophanes' *Ecclesiazusae*," 65.

34. Saxonhouse, "Comedy in Callipolis," 890. See also her discussion of authors who interpret Plato's dialogues as works which have to be read with an eye on their comedic elements (889n3).

35. See also Friedrich Nietzsche, *Beyond Good and Evil*, part 9, section 259, where Nietzsche posits that exploitation is at the heart of nature. The principle of equality, in

Plato and in Aristophanes, supports this view, because the harder the comedic or the dialogical characters try to institute equality, the more exploitative life becomes. See Nietzsche's *Beyond Good and Evil,* in *Basic Writings of Nietzsche*, trans. and ed. Walter Kaufmann (New York: Modern Library, 2000).

Chapter 3

1. Strauss, *Socrates and Aristophanes*, 111.

2. Jeffrey Henderson, "Introduction" to Aristophanes, *Acharnians, Knights*, trans. and ed. Jeffrey Henderson (Cambridge, MA: Harvard University Press, 1998), 220. All references to and quotations of the English text of the *Knights* are to Henderson's translation of that play. Where the English text differs from Henderson, the translation is by the author.

3. Henderson, *Acharnians. Knights*, 220.

4. Thucydides, *Landmark Thucydides*, 4.20, 234. For the strategic role of battles at Pylos see 4.1–41.

5. Thucydides, *Landmark Thucydides*, 4.20, 234.

6. Henderson, *Acharnians. Knights*, 220. On the historical significance of and Cleon's role in the Pylos affair, see Harriet I. Flower, "Thucydides and the Pylos Debate (4.27–29)," *Historia: Zeitschrift für Alte Geschichte.* Bd. 41, H. 1 (1992): 40–57. On Cleon's opposition to Pericles, Cleon's prosecution of Pericles, and Cleon's rule after Pericles's death, see Philip Yorke Earl of Hardwicke, *Athenian Letters: Or, The Epistolary Correspondence of an Agent of the King of Persia, Residing at Athens During the Peloponnesian War. Volume I.* (London: T. Cadell and W. Davies Publishing, 1810), I. 26, 94, 221.

7. Henderson, *Acharnians. Knights*, 221.

8. Everitt, *The Rise of Athens*, 277. See Aristotle's description of Cleon's vile character and poor form in giving public speeches in *The Athenian Constitution. The Eudemian Ethics. On Virtues and Vices*, trans. Harris Rackham (Cambridge, MA: Harvard University Press, 1935/1981), 28.3, 83. On Cleon's legacy in Aristophanes see Dorey, "Aristophanes and Cleon." Consult also A. G. Woodhead, "Thucydides' Portrait of Cleon," *Mnemosyne*, Fourth Series 13, no. 4 (1960): 289–317; Carl A. Anderson, "Themistocles and Cleon in Aristophanes' Knights," *American Journal of Philology* 110, no. 1 (1989): 10–16.

9. The metaphor of the ship of state appears also in Alcaeus, *Fragments of Old Comedy, Volume I Alcaeus to Diocles*, trans. Ian C. Storey (Cambridge, MA: Harvard University Press, 2011), Fr. 6, 208, 249; Sophocles, *Antigone*, trans. Richard Emil Brown (Oxford: Oxford University Press, 1989), 201–4; and somewhat less clearly in Aeschylus, *I, Persians. Seven against Thebes. Suppliants. Prometheus Bound*, trans. Alan H. Sommerstein (Cambridge, MA: Harvard University Press, 2009), 597–624.

10. Cleon is referred to by his first name only once in the play, at 976, by the Chorus of the Athenian knights.

11. Henderson, *Acharnians. Knights*, 222.

12. Henderson, *Acharnians. Knights*, 221.

13. Lowell Edmunds, *Cleon, Knights, and Aristophanes' Politics* (Lanham: University Press of America, 1987), 6 and 6n4, where Edmunds reads the identity of the slave in the *Knights* as Nicias "Contra: Dover 1959. Pro: Sommerstein 1980." In *Socrates and Aristophanes*, Strauss claims the slaves are "in fact the generals Demosthenes and Nikias" (80). However, see also Henderson, who proposes that the slaves' "characterization suggests rather that they represent the political 'outs' more generally" (222).

14. William Arrowsmith, "Aristophanes' *Knights*, Prologue," *Arion: A Journal of Humanities and the Classics* 1, no. 1 (1962): 79–94, 79.

15. Aristotle, in the *Politics*, credits Pericles with the establishment of jury duty pay; see his *Politics,* trans. Harris Rackham (Cambridge, MA: Harvard University Press, 1932), 1274a8. This opened the door to cases of bribery at court. In Plato's *Apology*, for example, Socrates hints that the three accusers bribed some of the jurymen to swing the vote. See Plato, *Apology*, in *Four Texts on Socrates: Plato's Euthyphro, Apology of Socrates, Crito, and Aristophanes' Clouds,* trans. Thomas G. West and Grace Starry West (Ithaca, NY: Cornell University Press, 1998), 36a–b. See also M. M. Markle, "Jury Pay and Assembly Pay at Athens," *History of Political Thought* no. 6½ (1985): 265–97; and Claire Taylor, "Bribery in Athenian Politics, Part II: Ancient Reaction and Perceptions," *Greece & Rome* 48, no. 2 (2001): 154–72.

16. Compare to *Gorgias* (464c–465d) and to *Republic* (372c–374a).

17. Strauss, *Socrates and Aristophanes*, 80.

18. On the subject of the meaning and significance of *desis* in ancient Greek drama, see Davis, *The Poetry of Philosophy*.

19. John E. Zimmerman, *Dictionary of Classical Mythology* (New York: Harper and Row, 1966), 169.

20. Zimmerman, *Dictionary of Classical Mythology*, 169.

21. See the *Knights* lines 282–84 (nt. 53), 656–81, 714–18, 812–19, 825–27, 1100–1106, 1166–95, and 1214–25. Foodstuffs and metaphors that rely on images and the use of food appear throughout the *Republic.*

22. In this context and in relation to our contemporary practices of public opinion shaping, it is instructive to consider the life and work of Edward Bernays, which is discussed by Larry Tye in his book, *The Father of Spin: Edward L. Bernays and the Birth of Public Relations* (London: Picador Press, 2002).

23. See also the chained prisoners in Plato's image of the Cave (514a–518e).

24. See also the passage in Plato's *Statesman* (267e–268b) where the discussion of herding animals gives way to the description of enchanted human beings. See further Michael Naas's take on shepherding in *Plato and the Invention of Life* (New York: Fordham University Press, 2018), 73–97.

25. In the *Apology*, Socrates insists that he neither educated human beings (33a) nor addressed them as politicians and rhetoricians do, but spoke to each privately (31b). Larry J. Bennet and William Blake Tyrrell, the authors of "Making Sense of Aristophanes' 'Knights,'" arrive at a diametrically opposite conclusion (from mine) about the culpability of Demos in the *Knights*. See their analyses in *Arethusa* 23, no. 2 (1990): 235–54.

26. Sean Braswell recommends a similar conclusion on the basis of his analysis of the relationship between the Athenian demos and Cleon in "Taking on a Demagogue Who Promised to Make Athens Great Again," Ozy: A Modern Media Company, https://www.ozy.com/2016.

27. See Plato's political metaphors in Melissa Lane, *Method and Politics in Plato's Statesman* (Cambridge: Cambridge University Press, 1998). See also Mitchell Miller, *The Philosopher in Plato's Statesman* (Boston: Martinus Nijhoff, 1980); and Michael Naas, *Plato and the Invention of Life*, who all understand weaving in the *Statesman*, for example, as a genuine model for rule and not as yet another metaphor for the faults that certain modes of ruling exhibit. According to my view, Plato ultimately dismisses weaving as a paradigm for rule.

28. See the *Republic* lines 487a, 489e, 490a–b, 490c–d, 492a, 494a–b, 495b–c, 498a–b, 501b, 502e–504a, 504e–507b.

29. Henderson remarks that the "hemp seller" and the "sheep seller" are "Eucrates of Melite, who had been a general in 432/1 and went on to have a long political career," and "Lysicles, who lived with Aspasia after Pericles' death and fell in battle in 428" (247nn10–11). Lysicles died in a battle with the Carians in 428 (Thucydides, *The History of the Peloponnesian War*, 3.19).

30. Nails in *The People of Plato* indicates the reasons why Thrasymachus's wild anger against Socrates, who talks about justice, might be at least partially justifiable. She describes Thrasymachus as "a diplomat in Athens on behalf of Chalcedon," and it was in this role that his "rhetorical skills were tested most significantly" (289). Thrasymachus's self-possession was also put to the test because he argued against Socrates at the house of Cephalus in Athens after "Chalcedon had mounted an unsuccessful revolt against imperial Athens" (289). Thrasymachus had his reasons to be upset and to scoff at Socrates's defense of just measures in politics. However, Arnaldo Momigliano disagrees that we can attribute the epithet "imperial" to the Athens of Plato's time. In *Alien Wisdom: The Limits of Hellenization* (Cambridge: Cambridge University Press, 1993), he writes that the "very word imperialism is modern; I do not know of any serious attempt to grasp the dynamics of any imperialism—old or new—before J. A. Hobson's *Imperialism* in 1920. If I am wrong, I am wrong in the company of comrade Vladimir Ilyich Ulyanov, who took the same view in his book on *Imperialism, the Highest Stage of Capitalism*" (27–28).

31. Benardete offered this alignment between the city and its *politeia* in his spring 1993 lectures on Aristotle's *De anima.*

32. Nails's remarks about Glaucon's character and history are illuminating (*People of Plato*, 154–56).

33. I part ways with authors like Howland who assume a more charitable interpretation of the simple city. Howland takes it to be the "True City" and observes that it "would seem to be Socrates'" (*Glaucon's Fate*, 255n6). In the context of animal—and especially pig—sacrifice, it is interesting to think of Burkert's view in *Homo Necans* (256–64). Further elucidation of the matter and its philosophical significance is offered by Rachel Barney, "Platonism, Moral Nostalgia, and the 'City of Pigs,'" *Proceedings of the Boston Area Colloquium in Ancient Philosophy* 27, no. 1 (2001): 207–27.

34. Thucydides, *The History of the Peloponnesian War*, 4.21–23.

35. Thucydides, *Landmark Thucydides*, 4.28.

36. Thucydides, *Landmark Thucydides*, 4.28.

37. Thucydides, *Landmark Thucydides*, 4.28.

38. Nails describes the violence in the wake of the aftermath of the Peloponnesian War as a "religious hysteria" ("Tragedy Off-Stage," 200). In the *Apology*, Plato has Socrates relate one unseemly episode that showcases terror in Athenian politics (32c–e).

39. Strauss, *Socrates and Aristophanes*, 92.

40. Strauss, *Socrates and Aristophanes*, 92.

41. There is some speculation on the subject of the ending of the *Knights* in John Williams White, "The Stage in Aristophanes," *Harvard Studies in Classical Philosophy* 2 (1891): 159–205, 184. See that same work on inconsistencies in the ascription of certain lines to the chorus (199n1).

42. See Strauss, *Socrates and Aristophanes*, 103.

43. See Strauss, *Socrates and Aristophanes*, 105.

44. Ian C. Storey offers helpful analyses of homosexuality in Aristophanes's plays in "Poets, Politicians and Perverts: Personal Humor in Aristophanes," *Classics Ireland* 5 (1998): 85–134, esp. 117–18.

45. If we assume that the *Banqueters*, which may have won Aristophanes the second place in 427 B.C.E., was the first comedy he produced, then the *Knights*, which came out in 424 B.C.E. and won the first prize at the Lenaea, is only three years later. Gilbert Norwood reports that in the *Babylonians* (426 B.C.E.) Aristophanes's scathing ridicule of Athenian politics and his critique "must have gone far (as we may well deduce from Cleon's wrath and from the famous speech in the *Acharnians*)" ("The *Babylonians* of Aristophanes," 3). It is then, partially, because of Cleon's outbursts against Aristophanes after the *Babylonians*, but also after the *Acharnians* (425 B.C.E.), that Aristophanes gave Cleon such a harsh treatment in the *Knights*. See further Helene P. Foley, who writes in "Tragedy and Politics in Aristophanes' *Acharnians*" that Aristophanes's

> second play, *Babylonians* [426], included an attack on state offices and politicians and, probably, the city's treatment of its allies. According to the scholia of *Acharnians* [425], the play provoked Cleon to indict Aristophanes (or the play's producer Callistratus) for [*adikia*] . . . and [*hubris*] . . . towards the [*demos*] . . . and the [*boule*] . . . on the grounds that he treasonably embarrassed the city before strangers at the City Dionysia. Cleon may also have questioned Aristophanes' citizenship, suggesting that the poet (or Callistratus) was really a native Aiginetan, not a true Athenian. Aristophanes returned fire at the Lenaia of 425 with *Acharnians*, a play that renews *Babylonians'* attack on Athens' misguided politics and politicians. Even more important, by making a separate peace with Sparta and by offering in his speech of self-defense before the chorus to defend the enemy, the comic hero Dikaiopolis commits 'crimes' equivalent to those for which Aristophanes was indicted (33).

46. "Making the Aristophanic Audience," *American Journal of Philology* 120, no. 3 (1999): 351–68, 360.

47. In the *Republic*, we get the obverse side of this image, where at 495b–c, Socrates claims that those who are best suited to study philosophy "leave her abandoned and unconsummated."

Chapter 4

1. Michel Foucault, *The Courage of the Truth: The Government of Self and Others II, Lectures at the Collège de France, 1983–1984*, ed. Frédéric Gros, François Ewald, Alessandro Fontana, and Arnold I. Davidson, trans. Graham Burchell (London: Palgrave Macmillan, 2011), 23–32.

2. René Descartes, *Meditations on First Philosophy*, trans. George Heffernan (South Bend, IN: University of Notre Dame Press, 2003), 75.

3. Consider Descartes's conclusion in the "Sixth Meditation" that the connection between the "I" of Descartes and his body is much more intimate than that between the sailors and their ship (*Meditations*, 201). There is another ambiguity in Descartes's use of language that has serious repercussions for our understanding of his meaning, namely, Descartes's incessant wavering between the "mind" and the "soul." Examples of his use of both terms, but without clarification as to their particularity in a given context, can be found throughout the *Meditations*.

4. Descartes, *Meditaitons*, 71.

5. "Le bon sens" is the phrase with which Descartes opens his French language edition of the *Discourse. Discours de la Méthod* (Cambridge: Cambridge University Press, 1923/2013), 1. I also consult the *Discourse on Method*, Richard Kennington (Newburyport: Focus Publishing, 2007), 15.

6. Descartes, *Discours de la méthode*, 16.

7. Descartes, *Discours de la méthode*, 17.

8. Descartes, *Discours de la méthode*, 17.

9. Descartes, *Discours de la méthode*, 17

10. Descartes, *Discours de la méthode*, 16.

11. The same idea is restated again, but now with an eye on the benefits or harms that those who *possess* the "best nature" can bestow upon the city (*Republic* 495a–b).

12. Consult Davis's commentary on Aristotle's *Poetics* (in Aristotle, *On Poetics*), which is instructive on the subject of the philosophical significance and compositional importance of characters. (1) "Story [*muthos*], then, is the first principle [*archê*] and like [*hoion*] the soul [*psychê*] of tragedy, and characters are second" (1450a38). (2) "The story [*muthos*] is the imitation of the action [*praxeôs*], and thought [*dianoia*] and character [*êthos*] are by nature the two causes of actions" (1450a3). (3) "Tragedy is an imitation, not of human beings, but of actions [*praxeôn*] and life [*biou*]" (1450a16), and "therefore, they do not act in order to imitate characters [*êthê*], but they include [or put together, *sumperilambanousin*] characters because of actions" (1450a21).

I analyze these passages, place them side by side, and get the following: story, in being likened to the soul, is the moving principle of the tragic work. Indeed, Aristotle states that *psychagôgei hê tragôdia tou muthou*, or "through story tragedy leads the soul" (1450a34). Davis comments that *psychagôgei* "referred originally to the leading of souls into or out of Hades" (22n61), that is, to and from the invisible realm. The characters are images through which otherwise invisible actions and thoughts become apparent and are woven into the story, which both moves the spectators and is also the moving principle of the tragic work. Although secondary, and even dispensable (1450a25), characters disclose the work of imitation or imaging (of actions and thoughts) that the soul of tragedy—the story—accomplishes. The characters, then, are images within an imitation. They are those images by means of which we are both implanted into the imitative work and are brought closer to the possibility of "recognition" (22n62), whether we are considering the events of tragedy or the circumstances of life. See also the excellent note on Aristotle's innovative use of *muthos* (Aristotle, *On Poetics*, 19n53).

13. In *The People of Plato*, Nails reports the following dates for Glaucon (429–382); Alcibiades (451–404); Charmides (446–403); and Theaetetus (415–391). See respectively, pages 154, 10, 90, and 274 for these dates.

14. Sallis, *Being and Logos*, 316. The *Birds* was produced in 414 B.C.E., when Plato must have been about fifteen years old.

15. All references are to Aristophanes, *Aristophanes I: Clouds, Wasps, Birds*, trans. Peter Meineck (Indianapolis: Hackett, 1998). When the English-language text differs from Meineck, the translation is by the author.

16. Aristophanes, *Clouds, Wasps, Birds*, 262.

17. Aristophanes, *Clouds, Wasps, Birds*, 262.

18. Strauss, *Socrates and Aristophanes*, 160.

19. Strauss, *Socrates and Aristophanes*, 160.

20. Strauss, *Socrates and Aristophanes*, 160.

21. Meineck attributes this line to Euelpides, but Hall and Geldart attribute it to Peisthetairos, in *Aristophanis Comoediae Tomus II*, trans. F. W. Hall and William M. Geldart (Oxford: Oxford University Press, 1907).

22. Zimmerman, *Dictionary of Classical Mythology*, 205–6, 259.

23. Strauss, *Socrates and Aristophanes*, 187.

24. Wayne Ambler opens his article with a bold but compelling statement of Aristophanes's intent. He writes: "The *Birds*' lead character is outrageous: he abandons his homeland, enlists allies, leads them in an attack on Zeus and the Olympian gods, becomes *tyrannos* over these same allies, does not shrink from grilling and basting some of them on his barbeque, and overthrows Zeus while securing for himself his right-hand girl, the beautiful Basileia," who as Ambler explains, brings with her "the stash of Zeus's powers, including his feared thunderbolt. But as outrageous as this Peisetairos is, Aristophanes is even more outrageous: the poet could have made Peisetairos into a grim or ridiculous reminder to other would-be tyrants, a defeated threat to Athenian democracy, piety, and virtue as demonstrated at Marathon. Instead," Ambler continues, "Aristophanes ends the play with this shocking character on center stage as a complete success." See Ambler, "Tyranny in Aristophanes's *Birds*," *Review of Politics* 74, no. 2 (2012): 185–86.

25. Howland, *Glaucon's Fate*, 13. On the relationship between Glaucon and Critias, see Nails, *The People of Plato*, 109–111, 154–56. See also Dan Dombrowski, "Plato's 'Noble' Lie," *History of Political Thought* 18, no. 4 (1997): 565–79.

26. Howland, *Glaucon's Fate*, 12.

27. Howland, *Glaucon's Fate*, 13.

28. Howland, *Glaucon's Fate*, 13.

29. Howland, *Glaucon's Fate*, 13.

30. Howland, *Glaucon's Fate*, 249n20.

31. Strauss, *Socrates and Aristophanes*, 187.

32. Circa 421–414 B.C.E. See Nails, *The People of Plato*, 115.

33. Aristophanes, *Clouds, Wasps, Birds*, 263. However, counter to my analysis of Socrates's method, see Anne-Marie Schultz, *Plato's Socrates as Narrator: A Philosophical Muse* (New York: Lexington Books, 2013), chap. 7, and esp. 177.

34. Howland, *Glaucon's Fate*, 139.

35. Strauss, *Socrates and Aristophanes*, 185.

36. Aristophanes, *Clouds, Wasps, Birds*, 264.

37. Euelpides vanishes at line 845. Peisthetairos, at that time, berates the priest who was in charge of the sacrifices that were meant to honor the establishment of Peisthetairos's reign.

38. Strauss, *Socrates and Aristophanes*, 163.

39. In the context of this question, it is advisable to see Howland's analysis of Thrasymachean tyranny in "Deluge of Desire" (*Glaucon's Fate*, 132–35) and his comparison of Thrasymachus's and Socrates's totalizing statements on injustice, justice, and rule (138). Howland concludes his remarks on the matter with the realization that given Glaucon's modification of the initial Thrasymachean view, Socrates must offer "extreme countermeasures in the war against injustice" (138). These measures set "the stage for the political arms race that unfolds in books 2 through 7—a race that culminates in Callipolis, in which justice and injustice ultimately converge" (138).

40. On this point, I part with Howland's analysis. He sees in Thrasymachus an honor-loving ideologue, but in Socrates, a genuine philosopher (*Glaucon's Fate*, 128–29). In fact,

the points that Howland lines up against Thrasymachus and for Socrates can just as easily be used to discredit Socrates. For instance, Howland tells us that Thrasymachus's "ideology is a kind of ersatz philosophy; it is not an erotic dialogue, but dogmatic monologue, and it requires political protection because it cannot sustain probing criticism" (128). However, consider that Socrates does most of the work of laying down the political constitution of the Kallipolis, which is inseparable from the rulers' philosophical pursuits. Furthermore, the "erotic dialogue" that Socrates has with any of his interlocutors may simply be seen as a less *thumatic*, albeit no less incendiary (nor any less potent) tool of persuasion than Thrasymachus's angered remarks. Socrates is better than Thrasymachus at the sorts of things at which Thrasymachus wishes he was exceptional and those things include indoctrination, political agitation, and an uncanny capacity to understand and use the psychological and doxic profile of the addressee for the purposes of persuasion.

41. Meineck suggests that "one cannot escape Athens, only re-create it" (Aristophanes, *Clouds, Wasps, Birds*, 264).

42. Nails points to a direct connection between the *Birds* and Socrates when "in *Birds*, a herald praises the utopian Bird City as revered among earthlings: 'Why, before you built this city all men were crazy about the Spartans: they wore their hair long, went hungry, never bathed, acted like Socrates, brandished batons' (1280–83, See also Chaerephon s.v.)" (*The People of Plato*, 268). Furthermore, Nails observes about "the choral *strophe* beginning at 1553 in *Birds*" that it "is also accusing" (268). Nails sees Socrates "in an underworld swamp, 'unwashed [as he] . . . conjures spirits' (*aloutous hou psychagôgei Sokratês*); the pun," Nails explains, "is especially fine, given the contemporary view of Socratic dialectic as *psychagōgia* (lit. *psychē*-leading; See also Teloh 1989, Howland 1993), but also because of its allusion to Aeschylus's *Psychagogoi*, a lost play in which Odysseus visits the underworld."

43. Arrowsmith compares the historical Athens with its tyrannical eros to the *Birds* and Peisthetairos, who "recruits the birds to a crusade against the gods—a crusade in which he will establish himself ultimately as a universal tyrant" ("Aristophanes' *Birds*," 131). David Konstan is another author who understands the play to iterate a "limitless imperial desire." See his "A City in the Air: Aristophanes' *Birds*," *Arethusa* 23, no. 2 (1990): 185.

44. Strauss, *Socrates and Aristophanes*, 184.

Chapter 5

1. Charles Griswold, *Self-Knowledge in Plato's Phaedrus* (Philadelphia: University of Pennsylvania Press, 2007), 223. Italics in the original. See further Marina Marren, "Against Simon" and "On a Wound by Premeditation": Lysias' Court Speech Writing Career as the Legal Background of the Phaedrus," *Greco-Roman Studies*, 59.3 (2021): 39–56. Jill Gordon talks about the *Phaedrus* and erotic poetry in her book, *Plato's Erotic World: From Cosmic Origins to Human Death*. (Cambridge: Cambridge University Press, 2012), esp., 102.

2. Aristotle gives a different alignment between tyranny, oligarchy, democracy, and their more desirable counterparts (kingship, aristocracy, and timocracy) in books II and III of the *Politics*. Yet another gradation of regimes comes up in Plato's *Statesman* at 301e–303b.

3. Griswold, *Self-Knowledge in Plato's Phaedrus*, 43.

4. Hesiod, *Theogony, Works and Days, Testimonia*, trans. Glenn W. Most (Cambridge, MA: Harvard University Press, 2007), 304–36.

5. Apollodorus, *The Library of Greek Mythology, Volume I*, trans. James G. Frazer (Cambridge, MA: Harvard University Press, 1921), 3.5.8.

6. See also Tanner, *Plato's Laughter*, 2017. Tanner takes Socratic guidance to have something to do with the realization that, unlike Socrates, most people are imbedded into and deeply attached to life. Whether such an attitude is preferable and ought to be emulated or whether it should only serve as a limit case—as a sort of measure against which we can examine our own attachments and their worth—for Tanner, Socrates appears as "a comical hero attached not to life itself, but to the logos" (18).

7. Thucydides, *The History of the Peloponnesian War*, 2.43.1.

8. Thucydides, *The History of the Peloponnesian War*, 3.3.37.

9. The passage, which I am paraphrasing, reads: *alla tyrannikôs en auto ho Erôs en pasê anarchia kai anomia zôn.*

10. Victor Parker, "Τύραννος: The Semantics of a Political Concept from Archilochus to Aristotle," *Hermes* 126, no. 2 (1998): 145–72.

11. Parker, "Τύραννος: The Semantics of a Political Concept," 152.

12. Parker, "Τύραννος: The Semantics of a Political Concept," 160–61. Sophocles's *Oedipus*, line 799, *hubris phuetuei tyrannon*, can be translated as "hubris begets a tyrant." I use the ancient Greek-language copy of the Loeb Classical Library edition: *Sophocles, Volume I: Ajax, Electra, Oedipus Tyrannus*, trans. Hugh Lloyd-Jones (Cambridge, MA: Harvard University Press, 1994). The English-language version of the text that I follow is Sophocles, *Oedipus Tyrannos*, trans. Peter Meineck and Paul Woodruff (Indianapolis: Hackett, 2000). Concerning tyranny in Sophocles's *Oedipus* as well as regarding the date and the original name of the play, see Marina Marren, "Sketches of Oedipus in Sophocles' Play about Tyranny" in *Logoi and Muthoi: Further Philosophical Investigations in Ancient Greek Literature*. William Wians, ed. (Albany: SUNY Press, 2019): 165–96.

13. Albert Einstein, "Why War? A Letter from Albert Einstein to Sigmund Freud," UNESCO, https://en.unesco.org/courier/may-1985/why-war-letter-albert-einstein-sigmund-freud.

14. Einstein, "Why War?"

15. In Plato, *The Complete Works of Plato*, ed. John M. Cooper and D. S. Hutchinson, trans. Dorothea Frede (Indianapolis: Hackett, 1997). I use the Loeb Classical edition for the Greek: Plato, *Plato 1: Euthyphro, Apology, Crito, Phaedo, Phaedrus*, ed. Harold North Fowler, trans. Walter R. M. Lamb (Cambridge, MA: Harvard University Press, 1982).

16. See Cinzia Arruzza, *A Wolf in the City: Tyranny and the Tyrant in Plato's Republic* (New York: Oxford University Press, 2019). Arruzza's analyses of Plato's *Republic* and, especially, of tyranny in books VIII and IX offer an understanding of the text that is akin to my own. Arruzza sees the *Republic* as a kind of diagnostic measure, which Plato offers to his contemporaries. According to Arruzza, Plato does not copy the tyrant of the *Republic* from any particular historical figure, but rather draws on "*poets, tragedians, comedians, historians, orators, and philosophers*" (14, italics in the original) and their presentations of tyranny when he builds his own image of the tyrant.

17. Nails reports that Plato's brother, Adeimantus, "fought at Megara . . . in 409, and was eulogized for it" (*The People of Plato*, 3). Despite this attribution to Adeimantus of military bravery, Strauss gives him a characteristic that bespeaks his intellectual cowardice. See Leo Strauss, *The City and Man* (Chicago: University of Chicago Press, 1978), 133. We should keep in mind Strauss's description of Adeimantus when reading the *Republic*. It qualifies Socrates's remark at 368a and gives an important frame to Adeimantus's speeches, as well as to those dialogical themes which get under way when Adeimantus has a say in the conversation.

18. On the oligarchy of 411 B.C.E., see Everitt, *The Rise of Athens*, 360–62.

19. Parker, in "Τύραννος: The Semantics of a Political Concept," discusses the possible origin and the modifications that the attribution "tyrant" and "tyranny" undergo. It is perhaps not altogether correct to think that the Persians were tyrannical rulers, especially toward their own population. Herodotus's *Histories* is dedicated, to a large extent, to figuring out whether and how the harsh Greek and Persian methods in politics and political corruption compare. It could well be the case that in the aftermath of the Persian War, there was much anti-Persian propaganda to which Socrates's character, too, resorts. The Greeks were far from being blameless when it comes to tyrannical rulers, as Mary White shows in her article on "Greek Tyranny," *Phoenix* 9, no. 1 (1995): 1–18.

20. Nails reports that Miltiades "served Darius I for a time, then joined the 'Ionian revolt'; when it was subjugated, Miltiades returned to Athens where he was tried and acquitted of tyranny in the Chersonese and promptly elected general in 490/89. . . . Miltiades IV is credited with a decisive role in the Athenian decision to fight the Persians at Marathon" (*The People of Plato*, 207). Nails goes on to say that Miltiades "dies of wounds, but not before the Athenians could fine him fifty *talents* for failure to capture the town. His son, Cimon II . . . inherited and paid the debt" (207).

21. Nails writes that "evidence is said to have emerged implicating Themistocles in treachery with the Persians. . . . Athens condemned him to death *in asbentia*" (*The People of Plato*, 280). See also Everitt's claim in *The Rise of Athens* that although the "Athenian *ecclesia* had elected [Themistocles] as general [he] . . . typically . . . bribed another likely candidate to stand down at the elections in February" (154). Nails also discusses Herodotus's take on the events surrounding the 480 B.C.E. battle at Thermopylae and writes that the Euboeans "had a word with Themistocles and offered him a bribe of thirty talents if he could persuade the high command to stand and fight. He pocketed the money . . . Themistocles never saw any harm in making a profit from doing the right thing" (167–68).

22. Nails offers a conjecture that "Cimon II was perhaps prosecuted by Pericles I for taking bribes from Alexander I of Macedonia in 463 or 462; he was acquitted" (*The People of Plato*, 97). However, she also writes about Cimon that he "arranged a five-year truce between Sparta and Athens. . . . Cimon II died in 450/49 while serving as general against the Persians on Cyprus" (*The People of Plato*, 97). Everitt tells us that "Cimon, the handsome young son of Miltiades . . . staged a demonstration to assert the loyalty of the aristocracy and its backing for Themistocles" (*The Rise of Athens*, 157) and his plan to rout the Persians at sea.

23. However, see Benardete, who writes, "Pericles might have used up inherited capital in a vain show." See his *The Rhetoric of Morality and Philosophy: Plato's Gorgias and Phaedrus* (Chicago: University of Chicago Press, 1991), 95.

24. On this subject, see Josine H. Block's "Perikles' Citizenship Law: A New Perspective," *Historia* 58, no. 2 (2009): 141–70. For sources on and discussion of *nothoi* and various forms of slavery, see Deborah Kamen, *Status in Classical Athens* (Princeton, NJ: Princeton University Press, 2013).

25. Everitt, *The Rise of Athens*, 77–78.

26. Everitt, *The Rise of Athens*, 77–78.

27. Everitt, *The Rise of Athens*, 77–78.

28. Everitt, *The Rise of Athens*, 77–78.

29. Everitt, *The Rise of Athens*, 77–78. Although Everitt quotes Herodotus, the latter disagrees with Everitt's assessment of the relationship between the Alcmaeonids and the

Pisistratids who, Herodotus says, "were driven out of power" by the Alcmaeonids—the family that "freed Athens." Herodotus, *The History*, trans. David Grene (Chicago: University of Chicago Press, 1988), 6.123.

30. Flickinger, *The Greek Theater and Its Drama*, 36. Flickinger also offers an analysis of the development of tragedy out of the dithyrambic songs to Dionysus (26).

31. Howland posits a different set of historical and literary prototypes for the tyrant of the *Republic*. He deftly contextualizes the meaning of Plato's appropriation of the "poet and singer Arion, who was forced by robbers to jump into the sea" (*Glaucon's Fate*, 48); Homer's "*Odyssey* [where] Poseidon whips up a storm that destroys Odysseus's raft"; and Sophocles's *Oedipus* by situating these against the historical events of the tyranny of Periander (155–65). The result is Howland's illuminating conclusion about Socrates's own philosophical efforts (both spoiled and successful) in the *Republic* (156–57). Demetra Kasimis offers another highly interesting and nuanced account of the problematic nature of Athenian democracy and Plato's reflections on it in the *Republic*. See her *The Perpetual Immigrant and the Limits of Athenian Democracy* (*Classics After Antiquity*). (Cambridge: Cambridge University Press, 2018).

Conclusion

1. Bernadete, *Encounters and Reflections*, 127.

2. See Jill Frank's book in which she argues that we need to attend carefully to Plato's poetic and dramatic art as a writer in order to understand the meaning of his philosophizing. Consult her *Poetic Justice: Rereading Plato's Republic* (Chicago: University of Chicago Press, 2018).

3. Aristotle, *Rhetoric*, line 1355a35, in *The Works of Aristotle, Volume II*, trans. William Rhys Roberts (Chicago: William Benton, 1952).

4. Benardete, *Encounters and Reflections*, 125–26.

BIBLIOGRAPHY

Aeschylus. *Persians, Seven against Thebes, Suppliants, Prometheus Bound.* Translated by Alan H. Sommerstein. Cambridge, MA: Harvard University Press, 2009.

Alcaeus. *Fragments of Old Comedy, Volume I: Alcaeus to Diocles.* Translated by Ian C. Storey. Cambridge, MA: Harvard University Press, 2011.

Ambler, Wayne. "Tyranny in Aristophanes's *Birds*." *Review of Politics* 74, no. 2 (2012): 185–86.

Anderson, Carl A. "Themistocles and Cleon in Aristophanes' Knights." *American Journal of Philology* 110, no. 1 (1989): 10–16.

Apollodorus. *The Library of Greek Mythology, Volume I.* Translated by James G. Frazer. Cambridge, MA: Harvard University Press, 1921.

Arieti, James. *Interpreting Plato: The Dialogues as Drama.* Lanham, MD: Rowman and Littlefield, 1991.

Aristophanes. *Acharnians, Knights.* Translated and edited by Jeffrey Henderson. Cambridge, MA: Harvard University Press, 1998.

———. *Aristophanes: Lysistrata, Thesmophoriazusae, Ecclesiazusae, Plutus.* Translated by Benjamin Bickley Rogers. Cambridge, MA: Harvard University Press, 1986.

———. *Aristophanes I: Clouds, Wasps, Birds.* Translated by Peter Meineck. Indianapolis: Hackett, 1998.

———. *Aristophanis Comoediae Tomus II.* Translated by F. W. Hall and William M. Geldart. Oxford: Oxford University Press, 1907.

Aristotle. *The Athenian Constitution, The Eudemian Ethics, On Virtues and Vices.* Translated by Harris Rackham. Cambridge, MA: Harvard University Press, 1981.

———. *On Poetics.* Translated by Seth Benardete and Michael Davis. South Bend, IN: St. Augustine's Press, 2002.

———. *Politics.* Translated by Harris Rackham. Cambridge, MA: Harvard University Press, 1932.

———. *The Works of Aristotle, Volume II.* Translated by William Rhys Roberts. Chicago: William Benton, 1952.

Arrowsmith, William. "Aristophanes' *Knights*, Prologue," *Arion: A Journal of Humanities and the Classics* 1, no. 1 (1962): 79–94.

Arruzza, Cinzia. "The Private and the Common in Plato's 'Republic.'" *History of Political Thought* 32, no. 2 (2011): 215–33.

———. *A Wolf in the City: Tyranny and the Tyrant in Plato's Republic.* New York: Oxford University Press, 2019.

Bakhtin, Mikhail. *Rabelais and His World.* Translated by Helene Iswolsky. Bloomington: Indiana University Press, 1984.

Baracchi, Claudia. "Beyond the Tragedy and Comedy of Authority." *Philosophy and Rhetoric* 34, no. 2 (2001): 151–76.

Barney, Rachel. "Platonism, Moral Nostalgia, and the 'City of Pigs.'" *Proceedings of the Boston Area Colloquium in Ancient Philosophy* 27, no. 1 (2001): 207–27.

Benardete, Seth. "Aristotle, 'De Anima' III.3–5." *Review of Metaphysics* 28, no. 4 (1975): 611–22.

———. *The Argument in the Action*. Chicago: University of Chicago Press, 2000.

———. *The Being of the Beautiful: Plato's Theaetetus, Sophist, and Statesman*. Translated by Seth Benardete. Chicago: University of Chicago Press, 2006.

———. *Encounters and Reflections: Conversations with Seth Benardete*. Edited by Ronna Burger. Chicago: University of Chicago Press, 2002.

———. *The Rhetoric of Morality and Philosophy: Plato's Gorgias and Phaedrus*. Chicago: University of Chicago Press, 1991.

———. *The Second Sailing: On Plato's Republic*. Chicago: University of Chicago Press, 1989.

———. "Second Thoughts." In *Herodotean Inquiries*. South Bend, IN: St. Augustine's Press, 1999.

———. *The Tragedy and Comedy of Life: Plato's Philebus*. Chicago: University of Chicago Press, 1993.

Bennet, Larry J., and William Blake Tyrrell. "Making Sense of Aristophanes' *Knights*." *Arethusa* 23, no. 2 (1990): 235–54.

Block, Josine H. "Perikles' Citizenship Law: A New Perspective." *Historia* 58, no. 2 (2009): 141–70.

Braswell, Sean. "Taking on a Demagogue Who Promised to Make Athens Great Again." Ozy: A Modern Media Company. https://www.ozy.com/2016.

Brill, Sara. *Plato on the Limits of Human Life*. Bloomington: Indiana University Press, 2013.

Burger, Ronna. *Aristotle's Dialogue with Socrates: On the Nicomachean Ethics*. Chicago: University of Chicago Press, 2008.

Burckhardt, Jacob. *The Greeks and Greek Civilization*, translated by Sheila Stern and edited by Oswyn Murray. New York: St. Martin's Griffin Press.

Burkert, Walter. *Homo Necans: The Anthropology of Ancient Greek Sacrificial Ritual and Myth*. Translated by Peter Bing. Berkeley: University of California Press, 1983.

Casement, William. "Political Theory in Aristophanes' *Ecclesiazusae*." *Journal of Thought* 21, no. 4 (1986): 64–79.

Charalabopoulos, Nikos G. *Platonic Drama and Its Ancient Reception*. Cambridge: Cambridge University Press, 2012.

Cohen, Beth, ed. *Not the Classical Ideal: Athens and the Construction of Other in Greek Art*. Leiden: Brill, 2000.

Cole, Susan G. "Procession and Celebration at the Dionysia." In *Theater and Society in the Classical World*, edited by Ruth Scodel, 25–38. Ann Arbor: University of Michigan Press, 1993.

———. "Under the Open Sky: Imagining the Dionysian Landscape." In *Human Developments in Sacred Landscapes: Between Ritual Tradition, Creativity, and Emotionality*, edited by Lutz Kappel and Vassiliki Pothou, 61–76. Gottingen: V&R Unipress, 2015.

Cornford, Francis M. *The Origin of Attic Comedy*. Cambridge: Cambridge University Press, 1934.

Cox, George W. *The Athenian Empire*. New York: Charles Scribner's Sons, 1887.

Davis, Michael. *The Poetry of Philosophy*. South Bend, IN: St. Augustine's Press, 1992.

Descartes, René. *Discourse on Method*. Translated by Richard Kennington. Newburyport, MA: Focus, 2007.

———. *Meditations on First Philosophy*. Translated by George Heffernan. South Bend, IN: University of Notre Dame Press, 2003.

De Wet, B. X. "Periclean Imperial Policy and the Mytelenean Debate," *Acta Classica* 6 (1963): 106–24.

Dombrowski, Dan. "Plato's 'Noble' Lie." *History of Political Thought* 18, no. 4 (1997): 565–79.

Dorey, Thomas A. "Aristophanes and Cleon." *Greece & Rome* 3, no. 2 (1956): 132–39.

Edmunds, Lowell. *Cleon, Knights, and Aristophanes' Politics*. Lanham, MD: University Press of America, 1987.

Einstein, Albert. "Why War? A Letter from Albert Einstein to Sigmund Freud." UNESCO. https://en.unesco.org/courier/may-1985/why-war-letter-albert-einstein-sigmund-freud.

Ellis, Hunter. "The *Ecclesiazusae* and the *Republic*." *International Journal of the Humanities: Annual Review* 9, no. 1 (2011): 177–86.

Everitt, Anthony. *The Rise of Athens: The Story of the World's Greatest Civilization*. New York: Random House, 2016.

Ewegen, Shane Montgomery. *Cratylus: The Comedy of Language*. Bloomington: Indiana University Press, 2013.

Flickinger, Roy C. *The Greek Theater and Its Drama*. Chicago: University of Chicago Press, 1936.

Flower, Harriet I. "Thucydides and the Pylos Debate (4.27–29)," *Historia: Zeitschrift für Alte Geschichte* 41, no. 1 (1992): 40–57.

Foley, Helene P. "Tragedy and Politics in Aristophanes' *Acharnians*," *Journal of Hellenic Studies* 108 (1988): 33–47.

Fortenbaugh, William W. "On Plato's Feminism in 'Republic' V." *Apeiron: A Journal for Ancient Philosophy and Science* 9, no. 2 (1975): 1–4.

Foucault, Michel. *The Courage of the Truth: The Government of Self and Others II; Lectures at the Collège de France, 1983–1984*. Edited by Frédéric Gros, François Ewald, Alessandro Fontana, and Arnold I. Davidson, translated by Graham Burchell. London: Palgrave Macmillan, 2011.

Frank, Jill. *Poetic Justice: Rereading Plato's Republic*. Chicago: University of Chicago Press, 2018.

Freud, Sigmund. *Das Unbehagen in der Kultur*. Berlin: Europäischer Literaturverlag, 2015.

Freydberg, Bernard. "Hearkening to Thalia: Toward the Rebirth of Comedy in Continental Philosophy." *Research in Phenomenology* 39, no. 3 (2009): 401–15.

———. *Philosophy and Comedy: Aristophanes, Logos, and Eros*. Bloomington: Indiana University Press, 2008.

———. *The Play of the Platonic Dialogues: Literature and the Sciences of Man*. New York: Peter Lang, 1997.

Greene, William Chase. "The Spirit of Comedy in Plato." *Harvard Studies in Classical Philology* 31 (1920): 63–123.

Griswold, Charles. *Self-Knowledge in Plato's Phaedrus*. Philadelphia: University of Pennsylvania Press, 2007.

Gordon, Jill. *Plato's Erotic World: From Cosmic Origins to Human Death*. Cambridge: Cambridge University Press, 2012.

Henderson, Jeffrey. "Introduction" to Aristophanes, *Acharnians, Knights*, translated and edited by Jeffrey Henderson. Cambridge, MA: Harvard University Press, 1998.

Herodotus. *The History*. Translated by David Grene. Chicago: University of Chicago Press, 1988.

Hesiod. *Theogony, Works and Days, Testimonia*. Translated by Glenn W. Most. Cambridge, MA: Harvard University Press, 2007.

Hildebrandt, Kurt. *Platon: Der Kampf des Geistes um die Macht*. Berlin: Georg Bondi, 1933.

Homer. *Odyssey*. Translated by Brian Kemball-Cook. New York: Calliope, 1993.

Howland, Jacob. *Glaucon's Fate: History, Myth, and Character in Plato's Republic*. Philadelphia: Paul Dry Books, 2018.

———. "Glaucon's Fate: Plato's *Republic* and the Drama of the Soul." *Proceedings of the Boston Area Colloquium for Ancient Philosophy* 29, no. 1 (2014): 113–46.

Hyland, Drew A. *Finitude and Transcendence in Platonic Dialogues*. Albany: SUNY Press, 1995.

Jaeger, Werner. *Paideia: Die Formung des griechischen Menschen*. Berlin: de Gruyter, 1933.

Janouchová, Petra. "The Cult of Bendis in Athens and Thrace." *Graeco-Latina Brunensia* 18, no. 1 (2013): 95–106.

Kagan, Donald. *The Peace of Nicias and the Sicilian Expedition: A New History of the Peloponnesian War*. Ithaca, NY: Cornell University Press, 1991.

Kamen, Deborah. *Status in Classical Athens*. Princeton, NJ: Princeton University Press, 2013.

Kasimis, Demetra. The Perpetual Immigrant and the Limits of Athenian Democracy (Classics After Antiquity). Cambridge: Cambridge University Press, 2018.

Konstan, David. "A City in the Air: Aristophanes' *Birds*." *Arethusa* 23, no. 2 (1990): 183–207.

Lämmle, Rebecca. *Poetik des Satyrspiels*. Heidelberg: Universitätsverlag, 2013.

Lane, Melissa. *Method and Politics in Plato's Statesman*. Cambridge: Cambridge University Press, 1998.

Lang, Mabel. "Cleon as the Anti-Pericles." *Classical Philology* 67, no. 3 (1927): 159–69.

Larson, Jennifer. *Ancient Greek Cults*. New York: Routledge, 2007.

Liddell, Henry George, and Robert Scott, eds. *Greek-English Lexicon*. Oxford: Clarendon, 1953.

Londey, Peter. "Perikles vs Thrace, 447 BC." In *Eleventh International Congress of Thracology* (proceedings from conference held in Istanbul, November 8–12, 2010), edited by Mustafa H. Sayar (2016): 159–64.

Markle, M. M. "Jury Pay and Assembly Pay at Athens." *History of Political Thought* no. 6½ (1985): 265–97.

Marren, Marina. " 'Against Simon' and 'On a Wound by Premeditation': Lysias' Court Speech Writing Career as the Legal Background of the Phaedrus," *Greco-Roman Studies* 59, no. 3 (2021): 39–56.

———. "Ascent to Αὐτὸ τὸ Καλόν in Plato's *Symposium* 204a–212d." In *Looking at Beauty to Kalon in Western Greece*, edited by Heather L. Reid and Tony Leyh, 133–48. Sioux City, IA: Parnassos Press, 2019.

———. "Plato and Aristophanes on (Want of) Education: Shame and Eros in Plato's *Gorgias* and Aristophanes' *Clouds*." *Ramus: Critical Studies in Greek and Roman Literature* 48, no. 2 (2019): 127–47.

———. "Sketches of Oedipus in Sophocles' Play about Tyranny." In *Logoi and Muthoi: Further Philosophical Investigations in Ancient Greek Literature*, edited by William Wians, 165–96. Albany: SUNY Press, 2019.

———. "State Violence and Weaving: Implications of Aristophanes' *Lysistrata* for Plato's *Statesman*." *Journal of Ancient Philosophy* 15, no. 1 (2021): 18–34.

———. "The Tragedy and Comedy of Tyranny: Plato's Symposium and Aristophanes' Frogs." *Philosophy and Literature* 44, no. 2 (2020): 207–25.

McCoy, Marina Berniz. "Plato's *Protagoras,* Writing, and the Comedy of Aporia." In *Plato's Protagoras: Essays on Confrontation of Philosophy and Sophistry. Philosophical Studies* 125, edited by Olof Pettersson and Vigdis Songe-Møller, 153–64. Cham, Switzerland: Springer Publishing, 2017.

———. *Image and Argument in Plato's Republic* (*SUNY Series in Ancient Greek Philosophy*). Albany: SUNY Press, 2020.

Metcalf, Robert. *Philosophy as Agôn: A Study of Plato's Gorgias and Related Texts.* Evanston, IL: Northwestern University Press, 2018.

Miller, Mitchell. *The Philosopher in Plato's Statesman.* Boston: Martinus Nijhoff, 1980.

Momigliano, Arnaldo. *Alien Wisdom: The Limits of Hellenization.* Cambridge: Cambridge University Press, 1993.

Moravcsik, Julius. "Inner Harmony and the Human Ideal in *Republic* IV and IX." *Journal of Ethics* 5, no. 1 (2001): 39–56.

Mossé, Laude. *Athens in Decline, 404–86 B.C.* Abingdon-on-Thames, UK: Routledge, 1973.

Naas, Michael. *Plato and the Invention of Life.* New York: Fordham University Press, 2018.

Nails, Debra. *The People of Plato: A Prosopography of Plato and Other Socratics.* Indianapolis: Hackett, 2002.

———. "Tragedy Off-Stage." In *Plato's Symposium: Issues in Interpretation and Reception*, edited by Jim H. Lesher, Debra Nails, and Frisbee C. C. Sheffield, 179–207. Cambridge, MA: Harvard University Press, 2006.

Nietzsche, Friedrich. *Beyond Good and Evil.* In *Basic Writings of Nietzsche*, translated and edited by Walter Kaufmann. New York: Modern Library, 2000.

Norwood, Gilbert. "The *Babylonians* of Aristophanes," *Classical Philology* 25, no. 1 (1930): 1–10.

Parker, Victor. "Τύραννος: The Semantics of a Political Concept from Archilochus to Aristotle." *Hermes* 126, no. 2 (1998): 145–72.

Parry, Richard D. *Plato's Craft of Justice.* Albany: SUNY Press, 1996.

Patterson, Richard. "The Platonic Art of Comedy and Tragedy." *Philosophy and Literature* 6, no. 1 (1982): 76–93.

Pickard-Cambridge, Arthur Wallace. *Dithyramb Tragedy and Comedy.* Oxford: Clarendon, 1927.

———. *The Dramatic Festivals of Athens.* Oxford: Oxford University Press, 1968.

Pierce, Christine. "Equality: 'Republic' V." *The Monist,* "Women's Liberation: Ethical, Social, and Political Issue," vol. 57, no. 1 (1973): 1–11.

Planinc, Zdravko. "Aristophanic Themes in Plato's *Republic*: A Post-Voegelinian Reading." *Political Science Reviewer* 41, no. 1 (2017): 1–32.

Plato. *Apology*. In *4 Texts on Socrates: Plato's Euthyphro, Apology of Socrates, Crito, and Aristophanes' Clouds.* Translated by Thomas G. West and Grace Starry West. Ithaca, NY: Cornell University Press, 1998.

———. *Euthyphro, Apology, Crito, Phaedo, Phaedrus.* Translated by Walter R. M. Lamb, edited by Harold North Fowler. Cambridge, MA: Harvard University Press, 1982.

———. *Phaedrus*. In *The Complete Works of Plato*, translated by Dorothea Frede, edited by John M. Cooper and D. S. Hutchinson. Indianapolis: Hackett, 1997.

———. *Republic.* Translated by Allan Bloom. New York: Basic Books, 1991.

———. *Republic, Volume I: Books 1–5.* Translated by Chris Emlyn-Jones and William Preddy. Cambridge, MA: Harvard University Press, 2013.

Plutarch. *Plutarch: Lives, Vol. III: Pericles and Fabius Maximus, Nicias and Crassus.* Translated by Bernadotte Perrin. Cambridge, MA: Harvard University Press, 1916.

Proclus. *The Commentaries of Proclus on the Timaeus of Plato, in Five Books; Containing a Treasury of Pythagoric and Platonic Physiology.* Translated by Thomas Taylor. London: A. J. Valpy, Red Lion Court, 1820.

Reckford, Kenneth J. *Aristophanes' Old-and-New Comedy, Volume I: Six Essays in Perspective.* Chapel Hill: University of North Carolina Press, 2010.

Rosen, Stanley. *Plato's Republic: A Study.* New Haven, CT: Yale University Press, 2005.

———. "The Role of Eros in Plato's *Republic.*" *Review of Metaphysics* 18, no. 3 (1965): 452–75.

Sallis, John. *Being and Logos: Reading the Platonic Dialogues.* Bloomington: Indiana University Press, 1996.

———. *Chorology: On Beginning in Plato's Timaeus.* Bloomington: Indiana University Press, 1999.

Saxonhouse, Arlene. "Comedy in the Callipolis: Animal Imagery in the *Republic.*" *American Political Science Review* 72, no. 3 (1978): 888–901.

Schlesier, Renate. "Mixtures of Masks: Maenads and Tragic Models." In *Masks of Dionysus*, edited by Thomas H. Carpenter and Christopher A. Faraone, 89–114. Ithaca, NY: Cornell University Press, 1993.

Schlutz, Anne-Marie. *Plato's Socrates as Narrator: A Philosophical Muse.* New York: Lexington Books, 2013.

Seaford, Richard. "Dionysus as Destroyer of the Household: Homer, Tragedy, and the Polis." In *Masks of Dionysus*, edited by Thomas H. Carpenter and Christopher A. Faraone, 115–46. Ithaca, NY: Cornell University Press, 1993.

Slater, Niall W. "Making the Aristophanic Audience," *American Journal of Philology* 120, no. 3 (1999): 351–68.

Smith, William, William Wayte, and G. E. Marindin. *A Dictionary of Greek and Roman Antiquities.* London: John Murray, 1890.

Sophocles. *Ajax, Electra, Oedipus Tyrannus.* Translated by Hugh Lloyd-Jones. Cambridge, MA: Harvard University Press, 1994.

———. *Antigone.* Translated by Richard Emil Brown. Oxford: Oxford University Press, 1989.

———. *Oedipus Tyrannos.* Translated by Peter Meineck and Paul Woodruff. Indianapolis: Hackett, 2000.

Storey, Ian C. "Poets, Politicians, and Perverts: Personal Humor in Aristophanes." *Classics Ireland* 5 (1998): 85–134.

Strauss, Leo. *The City and Man.* Chicago: University of Chicago Press, 1978.

———. "The Origins of Political Science and the Problem of Socrates: Six Public Lectures," *Interpretation* 23, no. 2 (Winter 1996): 127–207.

———. *Socrates and Aristophanes.* Chicago: University of Chicago Press, 1966.

Tanner, Sonja. *Plato's Laughter: Socrates as a Satyr and Comical Hero.* Albany: SUNY Press, 2017.

Taylor, Claire. "Bribery in Athenian Politics, Part II: Ancient Reaction and Perceptions." *Greece & Rome* 48, no. 2 (2001): 154–72.

Thucydides. *The History of the Peloponnesian War. The Landmark Thucydides: A Comprehensive Guide to the Peloponnesian War.* Translated by Richard Crawley, edited by Robert B. Strassler. New York: Touchstone, 2013.

Tye, Larry. *The Father of Spin: Edward L. Bernays and the Birth of Public Relations.* London: Picador Press, 2002.

Vickers, Michael. *Aristophanes and Alcibiades: Echoes of Contemporary History in Athenian Comedy.* Berlin: de Gruyter, 2015.

———. *Pericles on Stage.* Austin: University of Texas Press, 1997.

Vlastos, Gregory. *Plato: A Collection of Critical Essays 2.* New York: Anchor Books, 1971.

———. *Platonic Studies.* Princeton, NJ: Princeton University Press, 1973.

Waldstein, Charles. "The Panathenaic Festival and the Central Slab of the Parthenon Frieze." *American Journal of Archaeology and of the History of the Fine Arts* 1, no. 1 (1885): 10–17.

White, Mary. "Greek Tyranny." *Phoenix* 9, no. 1 (1995): 1–18.

Wilamowitz, Ulrich von. *Platon.* Berlin: Weidmann, 1917.

Wilson, J. R. S. "The Argument of *Republic* IV." *Philosophical Quarterly* 26, no. 103 (1976): 111–24.

Wolz, Henry G. "Philosophy as Drama: An Approach to Plato's Dialogues." *International Philosophical Quarterly* 3, no. 2 (1936): 236–70.

———. "Philosophy as Drama: An Approach to Plato's *Symposium.*" *Philosophy and Phenomenological Research* 30, no. 3 (1970): 323–53.

Woodhead, A. G. "Thucydides' Portrait of Cleon." *Mnemosyne,* Fourth Series 13, no. 4 (1960): 289–317.

Xenophon. *Memorabilia.* Translated by Amy L. Bonnette. Ithaca, NY: Cornell University Press, 1994.

Yorke, Philip Earl of Hardwicke. *Athenian Letters: Or, The Epistolary Correspondence of an Agent of the King of Persia, Residing at Athens During the Peloponnesian War. Volume I.* London: T. Cadell and W. Davies Publishing, 1810.

Zimmerman, John E. *Dictionary of Classical Mythology.* New York: Harper and Row, 1966.

Zuckert, Catherine H. "Is There a 'Straussian' Plato?" *Review of Politics* 74 (2012): 109–26.

INDEX